YOU'D BE NUTS TOO!

By Steve Brown

FOREWORD

Joining the army in 1993 probably saved me from going to prison, because as a teenager I was on a slippery downward slope. People who only know me from military service will be surprised to know that I committed crimes and dabbled in drugs before joining the army. "Second chance for teenage burglar" was the actual headline to a story about me in a regional newspaper, long ago. Day one of joining Parachute Regiment Recruit Company straightened me out, because I saw what real tough guys looked like and was in absolute awe of the paratroopers who taught us. Training was hard, and I struggled like everyone else, never being the best at anything but maintaining a good average. After completing six months of the toughest training in the world, I successfully joined the best regiment in the British Army, if not the world. During my career I was fortunate to meet some amazing people and make great friends with whom I shared good times and bad, eventually leaving the army in 2020.

In my last five years of service I underwent a substantial amount of psychotherapy after being diagnosed with PTSD. That therapy and the accompanying medication helped me understand why I have the emotions and feelings that I do, and how to cope with them. I don't claim to be in any way exceptional, we all have physical and psychological injuries that we have to deal with. Many times people have said to me things like "I haven't been through anything like what you have!" or "What happened to me is nothing compared to what you must have experienced!" I don't buy into that at all, firstly because they are assuming that what I've been through must have been horrendous, and secondly, because they might have dealt with it much better than me if they were in the same situation, we'll never know. I think trying to compare trauma, grief or any kind of mental illness is futile because it is totally individual, we all have different triggers, thresholds, and coping mechanisms.

This book is a collection of anecdotes and stories that have resonated with me either at the time or on reflection. Some are personal experiences, some are second or third hand accounts and I've retold them all how I remember them, or how they were passed on to me. Therapy has encouraged me to re-visit childhood memories, re-evaluate what is important and revise how I deal with day to day life. I have written a mixture of stories that include madness, sadness and badness that will hopefully make you laugh, cry, and shake your head in disbelief.

PSYCHOTHERAPY-

THE FACELESS SOLDIER

Holding on to the white painted, wooden handrail fixed to the wall, me and my brother crouched on the stairs and looked at each other for some reassurance. We had crept down quietly from our upstairs bedrooms to mount a rescue mission but not quite made it to the bottom, stopping a few stairs short as we listened to our mum who sounded terrified as her boyfriend attacked in flurries of violence. Cowering under the handrail close behind my brother, I could see the fear in his face as he turned to look at me, we were both crying, both scared, but determined to save our mum from the lunatic in our house. Hastily hatched at the top of the stairs our plan was to burst into the living room and launch an attack on this grown man so he would leave our mum alone, but the closer we got to the door the more the reality of the situation and likelihood of success sunk in. At that time, I would have been about six years old and my brother eight.

Suddenly, behind us at the top of the stairs a soldier appeared out of the darkness, a hero, here to save us. Dressed in World War 2 battle fatigues, he wore a steel helmet and carried a long rifle with a bayonet fixed. In the dark his face was indistinguish-

4

able, and he began to descend the stairs slowly and deliberately, carrying his rifle in one hand by his side, bayonet pointing towards the ceiling. My initial thoughts were that it must be my grandfather from my dad's side. He had apparently served in the war with distinction and was the only person I knew of from that era, but as he drew level with us, I realised it was not him and as the faceless figure went past, I recognised who it was.

This vision, which started as a memory from my childhood was part of an Eye Movement Desensitisation Peprogramming (EMDR) psychotherapy session I had with my psychologist, Dr Jackson at the Department of Clinical Mental Health in HMS Drake, Plymouth. The story was true up to the point of seeing the soldier and although it was sad to recollect the fear that my brother and I experienced and the suffering my mother had endured, my emotions only overwhelmed me when the significance of the faceless soldier dawned on me. Despite my resistance I began to cry through my closed eyes, tears dripping onto the carpet beneath me as I sat, leaning forward with my head in my hands. To this day I do not know if Dr Jackson already knew, or whether she expected the soldier to represent someone else when she asked me.

"Who is this soldier that has come to help you and your brother rescue your mum?"

There was a pause before I answered. "It's me." I said quietly, sobbing pathetically.

I think deep down, a part of me knew straight away, but it didn't make sense. I never met my grandfathers and knew very little about them, so I was struggling to work out who it could be. Accepting that it was me made me realise how helpless I must have felt as that young boy. There was no one coming to help us, and I knew it. The male support that I desperately needed was not only physically unavailable but also beyond my imagination, even in the form of a superhero or character.

-CHAPTER ONE-

WE'VE ALL HAD TO DO IT

ANGRY PIRATES

In Depot Para, Physical Training Instructors (PTI's) are the bane of your life that beast you every single time you encounter them. The mere mention of their name will send a shiver down your spine because you associate them with torment and suffering. For the most part, it's not personal, they're just doing their job, getting you to the peak of physical fitness, but one thing is certain, they are not your friend. While at Training Depot for the Parachute Regiment, our PTI, a Corporal from 1 Para crashed his motorbike. One of our Platoon Staff called us all into the corridor to tell us the sad news.

"Listen in you crows, your favourite PTI, Corporal Richards, was involved in an accident last night and, although he is alright, because he's a hard as fuck, super-nails, indestructible, paratrooper, his motorbike has sustained some injuries." He paused, pulled a sad face, and said, "Everybody say ahhhh."

To me and a few others it seemed obvious he wanted us to give a sympathetic "ahhhh," as in "ahhhh, that's really sad." But there were about forty of us there, and the vast majority had interpreted it differently and screamed "Arrgghhhhh!" like a bunch of angry pirates about to attack a treasure ship. I amended my sympathetic, soft "ahhhh" on the spot to join in with the others, still convinced I was right the first time and it quickly transformed from a quiet, subdued sound into a loud, angry snarl, "ahhhhAARRRRRRRRGGGHHHHHHHHH!!!!!! I screamed aggressively, at the top of my voice. It made no sense at all, but the instructor seemed happy enough and continued to explain the situation. "To fix that motorbike is going to cost £400! Corporal Richards hasn't got £400, but he needs that motorbike so he can get to camp to help you fuckers get fit and turn you into paratroopers." The sales pitch was short and sharp, but we all knew where it was leading. "If you lot wanted to help Corporal Richards fix his bike it would only take £10 from each of you to get it done. It's up to you, but I'm sure he would be very grateful, and in the Parachute Regiment we look out for each other." We all donated to the cause, even though we never saw any damage to a motorbike or got a thanks from anyone. Paying for imaginary items and things we didn't want was all part of Depot.

Once, I bought a pair of Nike running shoes from one of the Corporals for the bargain price of £5. They looked and felt just like the pair that I had previously owned before the "Locker Monster" stole them from my bedspace. On noticing they were missing I had reported to the Staff Office, slamming my feet hard into the ground as I halted outside the door.
"Who is it?" Came the shout from inside.
"Private Brown Corporal!" I replied loudly.
"Wait!"
There was a short pause while the Corporal came to the door.
"What do you want Brown?" he asked, looking me up and down as I stood bolt upright, arms against my sides and feet together.
"Corporal, I think the Locker Monster has taken my trainers!" I said sincerely.
The Corporal nodded knowingly. "Did you forget to lock your locker Brown?" he asked.
From day one we were told to always secure our equipment. Leaving things unattended was poor practice and would lead to them getting stolen or lost, and if you couldn't look after simple items like clothing or shoes, how could you be trusted with weapons or ammunition? Our instructors had even been kind enough to provide us with padlocks, albeit at an extortionate price.
I wasn't even sure if I had left my locker open. We were so busy running around like headless chickens, I couldn't remember. For all I knew, they had just opened it with the key.
"I think so Corporal yes." I said.

"Well, if the Locker Monster took them, they've gone. You'll have to get a new pair." He suggested. "I've got a couple of spare pairs that might fit you if you want to try them. What size are you?"

Back then, before my feet were smashed to bits, I was a size smaller than I am now. "Size 9 Corporal." I replied.

"Let me see what I've got. Wait there." He said, stepping out of sight momentarily before reappearing with two pairs of trainers, one clearly mine and the other belonging to someone else who would no doubt be along shortly to report them missing. He held them up for me to select.

"I'll take those ones please." I said, pointing to my own running shoes that I'd had for several months.

He passed them to me. "They're £5. You better try them on, to make sure they fit." He said. He was very professional.

"That's ok thanks Corporal, I'm sure they'll be fine." I replied.

"No, no, try them on first because I don't do refunds if they don't fit!" he insisted.

All I wanted to do was get back to my room and get ready for the next lesson, at any moment we would get called outside and be expected to be there within a few seconds. Being last was bad enough, and punishable by fifty press ups or a lap of the accommodation block but being late was inexcusable. I quickly unlaced my boots, put the trainers on, and went through the usual routine when trying on new shoes for the first time, pressing down on the the toes and sides and jumping up and down a couple times. "They fit perfectly Corporal; I'll take them please." I declared.

"Good. Leave your boots here and double away to get my money." He said, keeping hold of my black leather boots to ensure I would come back.

I duly returned with the £5 and paid. "Thanks Corporal." I said.

"Lucky I had them Brown!" he replied as I turned and ran back to my room. "Lock your fucking locker next time!" He shouted.

Speed marching at the end of an exercise in Depot

ABOVE STANDARD
STANDARDS

Inspections during recruit training are a stressful occasion. The first one I was involved in was an impromptu cursory check of facial hair where one of the instructors asked us all to raise our hands if we didn't need to shave every day. A few blokes put their hands up and were quickly mocked for the pathetic, barely visible whispers of hair above their top lip or on their chins.

"Everyone here will shave every day! If you think you don't need to, you are wrong, and if you don't shave you will be beasted until your fucking eyes bleed!" he told us.

Everything was subject to inspection, either at a pre-determined time and place, or at any opportune moment. Facial hair, haircuts, clothing, boots, pencil, (sharpened at both ends) washing and shaving kit, water bottles, (filled to the very top) weapons, equipment, everything. Our first locker inspection was a disaster. We were issued all of the clothing and equipment we needed for the next few months, given a quick demonstration on how to iron, shown a picture of a perfect "locker layout" and told to ensure our lockers looked like that the following morning, or else! At that point I couldn't even use an iron, and neither could half of the others in our ten-man room. My mum had tried to teach me, but I rapidly lost interest and gave up within a couple of minutes saying something stupid like. "Ironing is for women, I'll learn when I need to!" The blokes in our room that managed to finish before midnight were the same ones that hadn't insulted their mums and learned instead. The rest of us ironed until about 0200hrs, then got up again at 0500hrs. We all failed anyway. Clothes faced the wrong way, bars of soap were wet, coat hangers weren't the correct distance apart and boot laces had twists in them. Some instructors would pull items out in disgust and throw them on the floor to help you remember which ones were unsatisfactory.

Our first room inspection went the same way too, with specks of dust being discovered under beds, dead flies in the strip lights and footprints in the polish on the floor. In the utility room our Sergeant took out the air filter and was infuriated to find some lint stuck inside. In the ablutions the Corporals found dirt on the underside of the plugs and water marks in the sink. Standards were set high and failing an inspection meant a re-inspection, usually an hour later, and that would repeat indefinitely until we passed. It didn't take us long to realise it was worth putting in the effort for the initial inspection and everyone started mucking in together to make the place immaculate. The night before an inspection, to avoid leaving footprints, we'd cover the highly polished floors in blankets, cordon off most of the sinks and toilets and some people even slept on the floor so they have could have their bed-blocks perfectly made already in the morning. Every inch of accessible space was cleaned immaculately with bleach, including the inside of the toilet u-bend and the inside of the window frames, but I did see someone taking it too far once, when I went into another Section's ten-man room just down the corridor from mine. I walked in there as one of the recruits was removing a light switch from the wall with a screwdriver. He started cleaning behind the plastic fitting, using the tip of the screwdriver to push a piece of tissue paper into the small cavities.
"What are you doing?" I asked. "There's no need to go that far!" Part of me was wondering if he knew something I didn't, and maybe we should all be doing the same.
"I don't want to fail the inspection. It's just in case they check here for dust." He replied.
I looked to the others in his room and the looks on their faces

told me that they were thinking the same as me.

"That is fucking mental!" I muttered and left. They never did risk electrocution to find dust. Even the instructors had limits.

One time during a weapons inspection, my Corporal was sat checking the gas plug of my rifle, and as he started boring it out with the cleaning tool, I realised that I'd forgotten to do it myself before handing it in. As soon as he inserted it and felt the resistance of the carbon deposits his gaze shifted up to me.

"Sorry Corporal, I haven't done the gas plug properly, I forgot to bore it out." I said dejectedly.

He went to town on it, pushing the drill-bit in and out and twisting it around before withdrawing it.

"Tongue out Brown!" he ordered, with a wicked grin.

Obediently I stuck out my tongue and he stood up, turned the plug upside down and tapped the black carbon out into a small pile on my tongue. Instinctively I closed my mouth and swallowed it, it was fair enough I thought, I should have done a better job.

"What the fuck are you doing you lunatic!?" my Corporal said, seemingly surprised. "Spit it out you silly fucker!" he commanded.

I was also surprised. What else was I supposed to do with it? "It's gone Corporal." I said.

He shook his head. "You don't eat carbon Brown, you fucking maniac!" he laughed. "Go and clean this again and re-show it when you're done. The rest is good. Get away!" he handed me back the gas plug and I went back to the corridor to clean it properly.

If you're wondering, it tastes like chicken.

CROWS LIVE IN TREES
AND THEY SQUAWK

In the Parachute Regiment, recruits are called "Joe Crow" usually shortened to "Joe" or "Crow" and being a crow means you are at the bottom of the pile who has absolutely no control over your life; you are at the mercy of the instructors. One day during recruit training, my platoon of about forty young men were outside, waiting for our next instructions after eating some lunch. Even mealtimes were anxiety ridden, and when on the training area lunch would be brought out to us, either in the form of a foil tray with sausage and chips or a large flask, called a "Norwegian" containing an "Airborne Stew." My favourite was always airborne stew which was usually a beef casserole that had vegetables and dumplings in it. The downside to the stew was the instructors would unceremoniously dump it into our mess tins with a ladle, deliberately spilling it down the sides and handle, which gave us even more cleaning to do. Years later, after attending a course with soldiers from other regiments I learned that they called it "Range Stew", but I preferred our version. Just like back in camp, eating was always rushed, and we'd eat as fast as we could, like a pack of wild, hungry animals. As a naturally slow eater, I'd try to get a bit of everything from the meal into me to ensure I got some carbs, protein, and fat. For example, I'd take a bite of chicken, then a handful of chips, then a bite of a doughnut then a mouthful of peas, and I'd always have one eye on the instructors to track their progress, because once they finished, they'd be shouting orders at us. Sometimes we'd get "lucky" and "ice cream" would get brought out for dessert. Strangely, the ice cream we got in Depot looked, felt, and tasted just like Lard, and the chocolate and strawberry sauces bore a striking resemblance to HP Brown sauce and tomato ketchup! The lard and sauces were always left untouched on the table because no one had the time to mess about with them, opening them up and spreading them would waste eating time. I learned quickly that food was fuel, the taste and presentation was irrelevant, soldiers need food just like a car needs petrol and a solar panel needs sunlight. I remember doing an inter-section eating race once where we took bites out of the lard and passed it to the person behind to do the same. There were eight of us per section, sat in a straight line one behind the other, and I was number six. The race started and the sections were neck-and-neck, each bloke swallowing his bite and showing an empty mouth, before passing the packet of solid lard to the man behind who did the same. I was sixth, and although I wasn't a maths genius, I knew that there shouldn't still be 75% of the lard remaining. It was down to me and the two blokes behind me, so I took the biggest bite I could, ramming that slimy yellow brick into my mouth and biting through the greasy mass. Chewing lard is funny to watch but horrible to do, because it sticks to your teeth and the roof of your mouth, making it really difficult.

This particular day after lunch, our Sergeant was probably extremely irritated to see we were not suffering for a few seconds and called us over to put that right.
Placing his left hand on top of his head, he signalled us to move to him and he backed it up with a call. "583 Platoon, on me!" he shouted. Obediently we all sprinted to his position and stood to attention in three ranks.
"Right, you fuckers." He began. "Where do crows live?"
"In trees Sergeant!" yelled the recruit he pointed to.
"Correct! And what are you lot to me?"
"We're crows Sergeant!" shouted the next nominee.
"Correct! And what noise does a crow make?"
"They squawk Sergeant!" bellowed another young man.

15

"Yes, they do! So, let me hear your best squawks you fucking crows!" He ordered.

With that we all started squawking like a bunch of absolute maniacs and he pointed to a dishevelled old tree about 100 metres away.

"Now fly over to that tree and squawk from the top you fucking crows!" he screamed at us. Turning around we started running, flapping our arms like wings, and squawking as we raced toward the tree and began climbing, with some of the nimbler blokes rapidly getting up high in the rotten old branches. People were falling as branches snapped or they slipped off, but everyone did their best to appease the animated Sergeant who continued to point at people and shout impatiently. "Get up there then! Don't be last!"

In the distance a car approached on one of the few roads that dissected the training area and when one of the instructors noticed it had a small flag on the bonnet, he started shouting at us to get down. With all the squawking and chaos, it took a while for the message to get round, but everyone got quickly down, some jumping from substantial height when they heard the urgency in the voices of the instructors, who were all now beckoning us down frantically. The approaching car was a visiting high-ranking officer and thankfully he had not seen us up the tree. If he had, and he'd reprimanded our instructors they'd no doubt have blamed us, and beasted us for getting them in trouble!

THE WORLD'S WORST STRIPPER

In Aldershot there were a few pubs that were exclusively for paratroopers. Anyone not a member of 1, 2 or 3 Para was not welcome. Women were an exception to this rule of course, but it took a special kind of woman to walk through those doors. One such place was called "5's, The Airborne Inn" named after 5 Airborne Brigade and that place was crazy! The walls were covered in Parachute Regiment photos, flags, drawings and memorabilia, the floor was covered in spilled booze, broken glass, cigarette butts and urine and the windows were blocked out by Venetian blinds so nobody could see inside. The first time I went there was on a platoon piss-up that had started in the block before heading into town.

As a new bloke I had been instructed to buy a crate of lager which the senior blokes were already drinking when I entered the room at the back of the accommodation block. Everyone was sat in a semi-circle on plastic chairs and the first thing I noticed was one of the soldiers sat cross-legged wearing a sparkly silver mini dress, a blonde wig and bright red lipstick. He also had a matching purse and wore stockings and high heels. I'd seen this bloke knocking around but not spoken to him much, just exchanged hello's a couple of times. He was a big bloke, over six feet tall, built like a 1970's wrestler with a handlebar moustache and big hairy chest. Nobody batted an eyelid or even mentioned it, but I was deeply concerned. In the middle of the room was a black plastic bin full of cold water and cans of beer. I took one and sat down.

"How old are you Brown?" asked one of the Lance Corporals called Todd.

"Nineteen Corporal." I said.

"Have you got a chick?" He quizzed sharply.

"Yes Corporal." I replied.

"Have you got a big cock?" he randomly asked next.

I was taken aback, not expecting that. "What!?"

"Get it out, let's have a look."

This was worrying! I was sat opposite a hairy, sixteen-stone man dressed like a cheap Las Vegas hooker, and seemed to be the only one in the room that was uneasy with the request. Thinking on my feet I joked. "I thought I was doing that in 5's later."

Todd pointed at me excitedly. "Fucking right you are! Good idea!"

In my naivety I thought I'd got away with it, everyone would forget I reckoned.

In town, the first pub we went into was the George on the corner of Wellington Street and Victoria Road in the town centre. As a new bloke I hadn't been in any of the pubs yet because I had toed the line and waited to be asked by the senior blokes. I'd been warned that going downtown without prior consent was deemed as being a "Necky Crow" and would piss people off. As we walked in there were two doors, one left and one right.

"That's the civvy side, this is the Reg side." I was informed, turning right through the door. There was no mistaking it, we were definitely in the Para Reg side, almost every bloke in there was dressed the same, including me, and the dress code was; Maroon Parachute Regiment t-shirt, blue jeans, desert boots and shaved head. Not long after arriving, one of the other Privates came over to talk to me. "H" was in A Company too, but a different platoon and had been friendly from day one.

"Don't look now." He warned. "But there's a bloke stood at the bar that's one of the hardest blokes in the Reg. His name is Scouse, and he will fucking kill you if you ever piss him off! The bird next to him is his Mrs, and if he catches you looking at her,

18

he will fucking kill you! Don't look at him, and don't look at her!"

I glanced across discretely and identified who he was talking about. He was a big bloke, and he did look hard as nails, but then so did most of the others in there. I'd already established that H was a proper wind-up merchant and always taking the mickey out of someone, so assumed he was just trying to make me feel even more intimidated than I already was.

"Okay mate, thanks for the heads-up. I'll keep out of his way." I said.

A couple of minutes passed before another soldier from A Company came to warn me. Like H, Adam had been in battalion for a few years and was one of the Senior Toms that knew everybody. "Listen, there's a bloke in here you need to know about." He said seriously. "He's probably the hardest bloke in the Reg, and he's got a really short fuse. Adam described the same person, and I could see he was telling the truth, looking out for me so I didn't get myself killed. "Whatever you do, don't fuck with him! Don't even look at him!"

I was now in that situation where you really want to look but can't, and luckily Scouse was outside my arc of view so I couldn't accidentally catch his eye. Inevitably the time came when I needed to use the toilet and unfortunately, he was standing directly between me and the door. Keeping my eyes and head down I carefully walked through the crowd, trying my best to move with confidence but not cockiness and managed to get to the toilet door without knocking into anyone or spilling their drink. Being a new bloke was hideous, I assumed that everyone else in there was some old sweat that was looking at me with contempt for being such a crow and wondering if I even had permission to be in the pub. Stood at the urinal it was much quieter than the bar, but the quiet was interrupted when the door opened and another man entered, standing next to me at the trough. Instinctively I turned to see who it was, and my heart stopped beating momentarily as I came face to face with Scouse, as he also turned to look at me. For an awkward silent second we looked each other in the eye before I slowly turned back to face forward, devasted that I was now shut in a confined space with this bloke I'd been told not to even look at because he was so dangerous. All I could do was hope he wasn't in a bad mood. To be fair, he probably saw the look of terror on my face and thought it was funny. I finished up and left, pronto.

After the George we went to 5's which had a much different atmosphere from any pub I'd ever been in. It was the kind of place where a member of the Hell's Angels would turn around and walk out, because it was too rough! I'd grow to love that place during my time in Aldershot, it was an awesome pub where paratroopers felt at home and could really let their (notional) hair down, but that first time was intimidating. Luckily, the Corporal that wanted me to get naked was not in 5's when I got there with a few of the others, and we got settled in with a couple of beers. The atmosphere was raucous, with people jumping around covered in spilled beer and singing along loudly to songs like "Delilah" by Tom Jones and "Daydream Believer" by The Monkees. A Corporal from another platoon noticed me and my mate John who were the crows of 1 Platoon.
"Get up there and dance you fucking crows." He shouted, pointing at a raised platform along the wall. John didn't seem bothered at all and jumped straight up, taking me with him, and started to dance. He was loving it.
"Get naked you crows!" Came a shout from the crowd.
John had his top off in seconds, swinging it around above his head.
I noticed a man looking at me angrily. "Get naked now you little shit!" He said.
Nervously I tried to dance like a stripper and remember seeing a couple of girls in the crowd. I thought they would be embarrassed, but they were not, and pushed themselves to the front to get a better view.
My top was off, and I was playing with my belt, undoing it slowly then taking my time on my trouser fly, pretending to be

performing, but just delaying the inevitable.

Someone reached up and grabbed my trousers impatiently, yanking them down.

"Fucking hurry up you crow!" They shouted.

I gave up the dance and quickly pulled my trousers and boxer shorts down to my ankles, standing there naked, gyrating embarrassingly. The lack of shock from the crowd was surprising, everyone just carried on as if it were normal. It was normal in there. Suddenly I felt a yank on my trousers, and I was pulled from the ledge by my ankles, luckily landing on my feet on the dancefloor. As soon as I landed a pint of beer was thrown over me from in front, and a hand slapped my ass hard from behind. Then, in shock, I jumped sideways when I felt someone trying to put a finger in my ass, then jumped the other way when someone else stubbed out a cigarette on my butt cheek. The next thing I knew someone else was yanking on my boxer shorts and managed to rip them off, before stuffing them in my mouth. Then as it all calmed down, I took the opportunity to pull my jeans back up and re-tighten my belt, before accepting my pint that one of the blokes had kept safe. Stood there, thinking it was over, that I'd done my bit, I suddenly felt a warm sensation on my leg and when I looked down saw that a someone was urinating on me. I Looked up slowly to see a man, much taller than me, standing over me, menacingly staring straight into my eyes, pissing on my leg. All of this happened in a matter of seconds. I was way out of my depth in there, all I could do was carry on.

Half an hour later I noticed Todd had entered 5's and was enjoying himself with a couple of mates singing and laughing. It was dimly lit and very busy inside so I hoped he wouldn't see me, but he did. Pointing at me, he seemed to glide through the mass of people that separated us like a hot knife through butter, and shouted when within a few feet.

"Get up there and get your kit off Brown!" He yelled, pointing to the platform I'd been on previously.

"I've already done it." I answered. "You've missed it."

Todd shook his head and laughed; he knew full well I was going to do exactly as I was told. He wasn't a bully or nasty, but he had an aggressiveness and unpredictability about him that made me nervous.

"Get on with it." He said, grinning as he motioned to the ledge.

Up I went and got naked in public for the second time in my life. My dancing was crap and my strip routine even worse, I bet nobody else even remembered either of my performances, just another new bloke making a fool of himself. This time I got down by myself and received a congratulatory slap on the back for my efforts. After a few pints we left 5's for the next pub, another classy establishment called The Rat Pit.

The 5's, Airborne Inn, Aldershot

-CHAPTER TWO-

IT'S NOT ALL FUN
AND GAMES

GUNS ARE DANGEROUS

My first live-firing exercise in 3 Para was a two-week package in Sennybridge, Wales, a place renowned for its inhospitable weather and terrain. It was January 1994 and I had only been in battalion a few weeks and still a complete Joe Crow, so I got all the crappy jobs like, doing dixies in the cookhouse (cleaning pots and plates,) guard duty and fire piquet duty. Being the new bloke is a nightmare, you not only get the shit jobs, but you are also the first port of call for entertainment when the older soldiers get bored. One of the blokes I went through training with had been sent to the same platoon as me and we shared a room in Aldershot, John was one of the older recruits at 24 years old and came from a tough Cornish fishing town called Redruth. Built like a brick shithouse, with a head like a bag full of spanners, John was a living caricature of a paratrooper that couldn't spell anything with more than five letters or count to ten without using his fingers, but he was fit and strong and could drink and fight like a pro.

One day on the ranges, during a Company attack, our section was providing fire support to the assaulting section when everyone was suddenly ordered to cease fire. One of the experienced soldiers knew something had gone wrong and suggested someone may have been shot. They were right, a Corporal in the assaulting section had been hit in the back by a bullet and medics were on the scene quickly to sort him out. Nobody knew what had happened but over the next couple of days one of our Lance Corporals started winding John up.
"Why did you shoot Robbo John? What did he ever do to you? Why are you shooting at the other section? Who are you going

to shoot next John?" etc. etc. This Lance Corporal was very loud and very popular and before long others were making the same jokes when they saw John. I could see it was starting to wear on him.

"Ignore them mate." I said. "They're just winding you up. No one thinks it was you."

Robbo was in hospital recovering after surgery and was left with a large scar on his back, but eventually returned to duty.

A few days after the incident John and I were talking when he made a confession.

"I think I shot Robbo!" he said.

I was surprised. "Mate, they are only taking the piss! You didn't shoot him, it was probably a ricochet. Don't let them get to you." I replied.

"No, I know that, but I still think it was me." John said quietly.

I feigned a laugh "John, it wasn't you mate! Ignore the fuckers." I felt sorry for him.

John quickly checked that we were alone before he spoke. "The thing is, I was firing at the target and then, when I looked back, it started moving, then everyone started shouting to cease fire." He said worriedly.

The targets we'd been using were made of sheets of wood and hammered into the ground on stakes, they didn't move, and his eyesight was shockingly bad.

"Fucking hell mate!" I said. "Don't tell anyone else what you just said to me! Seriously, do not say that to anyone!" At the time I wasn't sure if the relentless banter had convinced him he'd done it, or whether he genuinely remembered the incident like that. Either way, my concern was for his safety. If he said that out loud, I imagined the other soldiers would beat the shit out of him. We kept that to ourselves and it was later determined, after an inquiry to have been a ricochet. John broke his back in a parachuting accident not long after that and ended up with a big scar on his back too. He was medically discharged.

During that same Kenya exercise, at the end of the six-week training package an officer was shot and killed on another live firing exercise I was on. It was the culmination of the live-firing phase and my first ever Battalion Attack. It was the night of the 25th of March 1994 and my platoon had only moved about 100 metres before the call came for everyone to cease fire and place their weapons and equipment on the ground where they stood. The previous few minutes had been very loud and intense as the Machine Gun Platoon fired over our heads and the Anti-Tank Platoon destroyed targets to our flanks. The lead platoon had begun to advance, and the point man had initiated contact with a burst of rifle fire immediately on seeing a target ahead. During night attacks, targets were often illuminated by a small white light so they could be identified and fired at accurately. At some point at the start of the advance an officer had queried his position in relation to the rest of the battalion and taken out his map to ensure he and his men weren't within the arcs of the advancing soldiers, studying it using the white light of his torch. However there had been a mistake and they were positioned directly in front of the lead platoon. The lead scout was an excellent soldier, well respected for his skills and when he saw the white light, reacted as briefed and engaged the target. The story goes that that burst of fire put a hole in one man's desert hat, another hole through the crotch of another man's trousers, took a finger from another soldier's hand and sadly also struck the body of the officer with the torch. Apparently, the officer raised the alarm by calling on his radio to cease fire and said that he'd been hit. Unfortunately, he died from his wounds.

I did my Junior Non-Commissioned Officer's Cadre in January – February 1998, known in the Parachute Regiment as "Drill and Duties" (D&D's.) Passing that course qualifies a Private soldier to become a Lance Corporal. A soldier was accidentally shot and killed on my course and the subsequent fallout from that incident changed the way ammunition was issued and accounted for in the armed forces. The days building up to the accident were extremely demanding as we marched miles across the boggy marshes and hills of the training area with heavy loads, conducted numerous attacks, patrols and ambushes, dug trenches and got very little sleep. The pressure was relentless, and people would fall asleep standing up if they stood still for more than a few seconds. Instructors constantly shouted orders and berated us for every trivial misdemeanour, and tempers flared between us paratroopers and the soldiers from the Guards Battalions who also attended the course. The way the exercise was planned meant that we started it using blank ammunition, then conducted some live firing, before going back to blank for the last part. That would prove a fatal mistake. The night we went from live ammunition to blank was the usual frenetic event. Soldiers rushed to empty all the live rounds from their weapons, magazines, and pouches into containers in the dark. Light was mostly provided by torches held in people's mouths as they used both hands to work and few people owned head torches back then. Hastened by the unrelenting pressure of the instructors, we made the required declaration that we had "no live rounds or empty cases in our possession" before being reissued the blank ammunition, which we loaded back into our magazines and pouches as fast as we could. One of the problems with blank and live firing exercises is that ammunition is constantly changing hands, because soldiers will run short at different times and rely on others to either refill their magazines or swap them for full ones that someone else loaded. You could quite easily start an attack with six magazines that you have stripped, cleaned, oiled, reassembled and loaded, and end the attack with four empty ones that are filthy, or eight full magazines that are rusty.

The final serial of that course was a blank-firing dawn attack onto a farm. Before first light we moved into position on the high ground above the objective and readied ourselves for the assault. First light came and we started the attack on the old stone walled building which was being defended by a group of recruits from the Guards Training Depot. As the attack progressed, my section was providing fire support to the section assaulting a bunker position outside the building when we heard the dreaded "Stop, Stop, Stop!" After a few seconds everyone had heard the call and it went quiet. It was still quite dark, the sun hadn't come up yet and everything was a kind of grey colour, but from where I was, we could see the soldiers and their instructor moving around at the bunker position.

The instructor shouted out urgently. "Medic! We need a medic down here!"

From behind us came another shout from the course commander. "What the fuck is going on? Pass the messages on!"

Realising the two couldn't hear each other, my section started to relay the messages between them, and it was quickly established that there was a man down on the enemy position who needed a medic.

"What's the matter with him?" came the question.

"He's fitting!" answered the instructor. "He's having a fit!"

An ambulance was called, and the exercise was called off while the casualty, was checked over. Identifying no wounds, the blokes took out a lightweight stretcher and lifted the young Guardsman onto it. Apparently, he was a very big guy and the blokes worked hard to extract him from the bunker position and get him up to the track where an ambulance would be able to access.

After a short while a civilian ambulance arrived, and the casualty was taken away to hospital.

Our course was over, and we were relieved, it had been a hard exercise. We cleaned our weapons and made brews while waited for the transport, and when the bus arrived, we loaded ourselves and our kit onto it gratefully.

The drive back to Pirbright was about 4 hours long and most of the blokes were asleep within minutes of sitting down on those comfy seats in the nice warm coach. I stayed awake, always preferring to keep busy during the day and save my sleep for night-time, even on exercise. After a few hours we were about

30 minutes from camp when one of the instructors received a phone call. Standing at the front of the coach he told everyone to wake up and listen in. The sleeping soldiers were woken by the others and everyone sat up straight to hear the announcement.

"Who here was on the assaulting section this morning when the exercise was stopped?" he requested.

Around the coach, several hands rose into the air.

"Who didn't have a BFA on the end of their weapon after the attack?" he asked cryptically.

One hand remained in the air.

"Well done dickhead, it looks like you just killed someone!" the instructor said before carrying on. "Right, we're turning around and going back to Sennybridge. That bloke who we put in the ambulance was shot, and he has died. The Military Police will be interviewing all of you when we get to Sennybridge.

The BFA was a yellow painted, metal Blank Firing Attachment that screwed into the muzzle of the SA80 rifle and enabled the weapon to automatically re-cock when blank firing. At the time they were not designed as a "bullet catcher" like modern versions, and an inadvertent live round would destroy it, removing it from the end of the weapon, but preventing the round from travelling any distance. If more live rounds were subsequently fired though, there was nothing to impede them once it had been shot off.

Sometime later we learned that Guardsman King from the Grenadier Guards, had been hit with a live round during the attack, as the defensive position he occupied was assaulted. It transpired that five live rounds had been mixed up with the blank ammo and one of them had hit him during a burst of automatic fire. The reason nobody had initially realised that he'd been shot was because there was no obvious bleeding or exit wound. The 5.56mm round that struck his body had stayed inside leaving only a small entry wound that had gone undiscovered but caused massive internal injuries. Because there were no obvious wounds it had been assumed that he was having a seizure or epileptic attack. The subsequent investigations and inquest into that incident resulted in the implementation of much stricter rules regarding the use of ammunition and its issue and receipt throughout the armed services.

TANDEM PARACHUTING
IS DANGEROUS

One of the courses I completed while in the Pathfinders was the Military Tandem Masters Course. To be honest, it was a course I never really wanted to do, because when I used to watch the tandem masters jump it always looked too complicated. Their equipment seemed way too confusing, with different handles and straps all over the place and far too much to remember during their practice drills. There came a time though, when I was the only person with enough freefall jumps to do it, so reluctantly I went. It was actually a very good course and I enjoyed learning a new skill and testing myself, but because of unforeseen events, that course was halted twice, and I would only qualify after the third attempt.

The first course was stopped when a problem with the parachute was identified and caused it to be grounded. One jump was utilised for us to practice deploying the main canopy with a secondary handle. This might be necessary if you sustained an injury to your arm and were unable to use the primary handle. I jumped, went through my drills and free-falled to the designated altitude before grabbing the handle and pulling. The handle stayed where it was which was surprising, but I had never used that one before so guessed it was probably a bit stiffer than what I was used to. I gave it a couple more pulls and it still didn't move. Even though I was falling at about 120mph, I knew I had plenty of altitude, so I reset into my freefall position, quickly shook out my arms and started again, grabbing the handle firmly and yanking it away from my body as taught. Nothing. It didn't budge. I'm not the strongest bloke in the world but I'm not weak either, so I abandoned that option and used the primary handle instead which worked perfectly, deploying a nice big silky parachute above my head. On return to the hangar, I learned that I was not the only one who had experienced that problem and of the four men on the course two handles had failed. After testing by the instructors and engineers it was agreed that there was a technical error with the parachute which required fixing, and the parachute was grounded.

Once the parachute was fixed another course was scheduled so that we could complete our training and we flew back out to the U.S. As we progressed, the jumps got more difficult and one night we prepared for a night-time HALO descent with a passenger and equipment. Fitted to an oxygen system, we'd be jumping from fifteen thousand feet with weapons, and rucksacks. Passengers during the course are volunteers, usually one of your friends or a Parachute Jumping Instructor (PJI) from the RAF. My passenger that night was an officer from the RAF Falcons parachute display team. On the same sortie as myself was a PJI I had known for several years called Jim, who was also a student on the course. His passenger was his best mate, and they were both experienced skydivers. I recognised his passenger because I had seen him in the gym earlier in the week when he was on the treadmill next to mine and going like the clappers! I'd sneaked a peak at his speed on the display screen and been well impressed, he was really fast. I'd even asked another PJI about him and he'd confirmed his name was Marc and he was extremely fit. Those two went out ahead of me and I watched them exit, quickly disappearing into the dark abyss, then waited for the thumbs up for me to go. My descent was nice and stable, and the parachute did its job reliably once more. Happy that we had a good canopy I removed my oxygen mask and began steering to the illuminated landing area which was easy to see in the darkness of the desert. Starting my landing pattern, I was heading downwind when I noticed a light come on ahead and below us. It was the internal lights of a vehicle. I spoke to my passenger. "See that vehicle with the lights on?" I said. "We'll start a steady 180 degree turn into wind when we get above that." I handed him the secondary steering toggle so he could assist with the turn and the landing. The lights were an excellent and unexpected reference point.

"Roger that." he acknowledged.

We got above the vehicle and initiated a slow deliberate turn and commenced our final leg into wind, towards the landing area. Dropping our equipment to the end of its rope below us I gave last instructions to my passenger to get his feet up and pull down on the steering toggles on my count. Our landing was ok, and we came to a halt sat on the dusty floor after a small slide on our asses.

Before we even had the chance to speak, a member of the RAF staff rushed over to us and informed us that there had been an accident and that Jim and Marc were in a bad way. Jim was conscious but Marc was not, and they were being treated where they had landed. After a while there were emergency services all over the drop zone including a medical helicopter, fire and rescue and ambulance. Jim and Marc were rushed to hospital where unfortunately Marc died from his injuries despite best efforts to save him. Jim suffered a broken back and the loss of his best friend.

One of my friends was on the drop zone when the incident happened and had witnessed them crash. He said they came in fast, in the middle of a turn and hit the ground very hard, with the mass of equipment clattering on impact with the hard-baked floor. On previous exercises to the desert the landing areas had been freshly ploughed, making them a very soft place to land. For some reason, on this exercise, only the daytime landing area had been ploughed and that was soft. We had previously joked that it was safer to land outside of the night-time landing area because it was not only hard baked like the rest of the area, but it was also steeply rutted, where it had set from previous ploughing. At least the natural floor was reasonably flat.

In 2006 my third tandem course went without any further drama and we held a remembrance service for Marc at a memorial in the American base, where his name was added to the other British servicemen that had perished while parachuting there.

MILITARY FREEFALL
IS DANGEROUS

Holding on to James with his arm over his shoulders for support Ash hobbled past me as I drank a cold bottle of water and watched some T.V between jumps. I hadn't noticed them until they were going past and checked with James. "Is he alright?" I asked.

"He'll be okay mate." James replied and sat him down on a settee before helping him lie down and lifting up his feet onto the seat cushions. At first, I thought Ash had probably twisted an ankle and was going to elevate it and get some ice on it, but after talking to James I found out he'd had a nightmare jump where he had spun out of control so fast, he'd gone unconscious in freefall. Luckily, by then, our freefall parachutes were fitted with electronic automatic opening devices, and his had saved his life, firing off his reserve parachute as he hurtled towards the ground at terminal velocity. I went to check on Ash a few minutes later and was shocked by his appearance. The first thing I noticed, because it was impossible not to, was the colour of his eyes. They were completely red! Not just bloodshot, there was zero white in his eyeball, they were totally blown out and blood red, like something from a horror film. He was still a bit dazed, but talking clearly, and he described what had happened as far as he could remember it. Military freefall, carrying a heavy rucksack attached to your body can be difficult to do sometimes. The equipment makes it harder to maintain a stable position, because it catches the rushing air and causes lift, which can flip you over or force you in to an involuntary turn. Ash had gone into such a turn, and unable to correct or counter it, it rapidly increased in rotational speed to a point where his arms were extended above his head and he couldn't bring them down to operate his parachute handles. He'd spun so fast, the G-force had stretched him out, causing blood to rush to his extremities and head and send him unconscious. When he came round, he was hanging below a parachute only a few seconds from landing and was lucky not to get injured as he still had his equipment attached. Not only were his eyes deep red, his head, hands, and feet were swollen too. He never lived that one down, because he already had a big head.

Later that day I spoke to Dunny, the Parachute Jump Instructor (PJI) who'd jumped with Ash, a massively experienced parachutist who'd done thousands of jumps and taught students how to freefall for years.
"Steve, I honestly thought he was going to die!" he said, which is not the kind of language you usually hear from the PJI's who've seen a lot of parachuting incidents and aren't easily shocked. Dunny told me how he'd held onto Ash for the exit and let go of him once he thought he was stable. Ash had started to turn, and Dunny had taken hold of him again to settle him down and give him instructions on how to adjust his body position. Instructions are given using hand signals during freefall, because you can't hear anything but the air rushing past your ears. Once happy that Ash was stable, he let him go again, and once more he started to turn. Dunny said that the first turn was slow, and he used hand signals again to correct him, but the turn got faster and before he knew it, Ash was starting to go pretty fast. Dunny tried to grab him but couldn't time it right and ended up getting kicked in the head, losing his helmet, and going unstable himself for a couple of seconds. When he sorted himself out, he looked for Ash and saw he was already well below him spinning out of control.
"He was spinning like a fucking propeller mate!" he told me.
Dunny tried to catch him up by falling as vertically as he could to gain speed, which is a difficult position to hold in freefall.

"I was on my fucking head, and I still couldn't get anywhere near him!" he said. "I've never seen anything like it, he was going so fast!" He leant forwards with his arms by his side to make his point and described how relieved he was when he saw Ash's reserve parachute open.

Personally, I have only experienced an involuntary turn during freefall a couple of times, and that was back when we jumped with our equipment on the backs of our legs. Luckily, I was able to control it by altering my position, but when it happens you can feel it "winding up" and it is a scary feeling. The first time was a night-time high-altitude, low opening (HALO) insertion onto an exercise, and the only position I could adopt that stopped me from spinning was, legs together, left arm straight out above my head, and right arm straight out to the side and I couldn't wait for it to end. The other time, I had to reach behind me, grab hold of my bergan and pull it up as far as I could. If I let go, I'd start spinning again so I had to stay in that position all the way down to pull height, then let go and pull quickly.

EXPLOSIVES ARE
DANGEROUS

After one of our teams identified a suitable location for a British Army base and we started to establish a presence, I was driving through the city of Al-Amarah, Iraq in a four-vehicle patrol, when a man stood at the side of the road began frantically flagging us down. Stopping next to him I used our interpreter to ask what the problem was, and he said that there was a large stockpile of munitions in a nearby factory that had been abandoned by the withdrawing Iraqi Army. His directions were too complicated to remember, so I asked him to get on-board and guide us there, informing the rest of the team what was happening, and to remain vigilant in case it was some kind of trap. We drove for a short while before turning off the tarmac road onto a dirt track, towards an industrial site. Cautiously we entered an area of high wired fences and large derelict buildings that showed clear signs of battle, with missing doors, smashed windows, and damaged roofs. Litter was strewn across the ground and blown against fences, and paperwork from inside the old offices was scattered everywhere. When the building came into view our guide asked if he could leave, because there were a lot of people ahead and he did not want to draw attention to himself by voluntarily helping us. He jumped down from the vehicle and we continued, moving closer to the building vigilantly. Sometimes the presence of civilians, especially children is a good indicator that an area is relatively safe from I.E.D's or likely attack, because the enemy might warn off the local population of a future attack or explosion, but not always. There were several people walking in and out of the buildings, most of them going in empty handed, and coming out carrying items of furniture, electrical items, or pieces of wood for future home projects. I noticed a couple of small motorbikes were parked outside, stacked high with huge piles of timber that defied the laws of physics, like something you'd see at the circus. Dismounting, with one of my blokes I walked towards the building that had been identified as the munitions cache, and quickly noticed a Russian, multiple launch rocket system parked underneath an open fronted barn. Reverse parked as far as it could go to conceal it from any aircraft or satellites above, the truck with its forty 122mm barrels, sat idle with the bonnet propped open and its engine pilfered for parts. Stepping through an open doorway we entered a large, unlit storeroom with wooden crates stacked fifteen feet high. Light was provided by the open windows which were high on the wall, and through these windows children and young adults were entering the building and clambering over the boxes, before using sledge hammers to break them apart, remove the contents, then take the timber away. The problem was not that they were obviously stealing, the problem was, the wooden crates were ammunition containers and held live rockets in them. As soon as I realised this I shouted and gestured at the young men and boys to get away, instructing my interpreter to do the same. They were raising their hammers high above their heads and swinging them into the boxes hard, seemingly oblivious to the dangerous situation they were creating. Strangely, the man who'd guided us there, but didn't want to be seen with us, had followed us anyway, and also entered the building. He too shouted at them to get out, brandishing a piece of wood and running at them to scare them off. If one of those rockets detonated it could cause a massive ripple effect and we'd all be obliterated, and we couldn't be sure there weren't chemical weapons there either. We cleared everybody out and reported the discovery to HQ who then tasked the Royal Engineers to deal with it. I did a rough count and there were at least 250 rockets in that room. Those people were so desperate for resources they were prepared to risk everything just to get some wood to enhance the structure of their homes or burn in their fires to keep warm at night.

Nearing the end of our Iraq tour we had some unused PE4 plastic explosives that we'd taken out of its packaging and couldn't be returned, so we used it to conduct some demolitions training before we left. An abandoned Iraqi Army camp in the middle of the desert was the perfect place to practice, and under the supervision of our Royal Engineer demolitions specialist we destroyed some artillery guns, cut pieces of metal, and blew up some RPG rockets and munitions in situ, to prevent them getting onto the wrong hands. One of the blokes, Bryan, decided to practice using an improvised "mousehole charge" which is a method of blowing a small hole in a wall that can be used as an entry point. Taking his time, he built the frame using a couple of bits of wood he found lying around and taping the explosives to it with black duct tape. Fixing it against the wall Bryan ignited the safety fuse and walked outside to take cover, and after the calculated time the safety cord ignited the detonation cord, which instantaneously set off the plastic explosives. Those buildings weren't exactly the highest quality of architecture or craftsmanship, and were already scarred with signs of battle, but when the whole building collapsed into a pile of rubble, we had to laugh. Instead of creating a small hole, the blast had caused the flat roof to fall down and all the walls to cave in. Bry joked about the origin of the name PE4. "P for plenty gents!" he chuckled. In summary: Great success!

STATIC LINE PARACHUTING IS DANGEROUS

Before a military parachute jump there is a lot of faffing around, preparation and rehearsals, and for those that don't like parachuting, all the build-up only adds to their anxiety. To be honest military parachuting is not all that much fun for anybody. You normally have an early start, a long journey on a coach to RAF Brize Norton, a brief about all the dangers of parachuting and the hazards on the drop zone, then sit around for hours in an uncomfortable parachute harness that weighs 40lb, before getting on a plane and sitting in a cramped position for hours with your legs wedged between rucksacks as the pilot throws it around while low-level flying. Eventually you are told to stand up, clip your heavy rucksack to the front of the harness and wait for the order to jump. Normally, this wait lasts about forty minutes and whether you like parachuting or not, you just want to get the hell out of that plane when the time comes. Men strain under the weight of their equipment as the plane hugs the terrain and banks sharply. Some vomit into bags, some on the floor as they sweat and curse. The discomfort that you experience during that forty minutes of standing up is hard to imagine if you haven't done it. Every part of your body is under immense strain. The parachute straps pull down hard on your shoulders as you hold on to the static line in one hand, the 40lb parachute pulling you backwards, and the 20lb reserve parachute pulling you forwards in opposing forces. Bergans weighing up to a maximum of 120lb also hang off the front of the parachute harness, just below the reserve parachute. During tactical flying a C130 Hercules aircraft can generate forces in excess of two G's, which means the force going through your muscles and joints is over twice their actual weight, so the average man, weighing about 75kg would be putting in excess of 300kg of stress through his body. During my time as a paratrooper, I heard a lot of people talk about the heavy loads they'd jumped with, sometimes subject to poetic license, but only once did I see a paratrooper turned away from an aircraft by the R.A.F because his equipment was too heavy to jump with. My kit was heavy, filled with radio equipment, batteries, and ammunition, and a few of the blokes had even come to lift it off the ground to compare it with their own, surprised at the weight. However, the bloke in front of me, a Corporal called "Posh Bob" had kit even heavier than mine. He was from the Machine Gun Platoon and when I helped him lift his bergan up to the PJI on the plane, it was such a struggle to move, they put it on the scales to weigh it. Giving it back to Bob they told him he needed to lose twenty pounds worth of kit or he couldn't jump. I had never seen that before but couldn't offer to take some of the burden because my own kit only just scraped through itself. I asked Bob what he was carrying to be so heavy, and he told me he had a radio, spare batteries, a machine gun plus spare barrel, and a box of machine gun ammunition. All this on top of his usual kit and rifle made his bergan weigh about 140lbs.

During rehearsals for one parachute descent onto Salisbury Plain, I noticed a young "One Pip Wonder" (Second Lieutenant) that I'd never seen before and asked one of the others who it was. It turned out he was from the Territorial Army (Reserves) and was attached to us for the exercise, so from a young paratroopers perspective he was pretty low on the importance scale. The next time I saw that officer was a few seconds after jumping out the starboard door of the plane. I propelled myself into the blasting air of the slipstream as dynamically as I could with my kit weighing me down, and called out my compulsory count

"One thousand, two thousand, three thousand, check canopy!" The low-level parachute (LLP) is designed to be operated from as low as two hundred and fifty feet, so it opens very quickly and when I looked up, there it reliably was. I took a couple of seconds to visually inspect the rigging lines and parachute were intact before lowering my gaze to check the space around me, but it was already too late. Immediately on looking forward I was faced with the rapidly approaching rigging lines of another parachute and before I even had time to react, I'd passed through them and dropped a couple of feet, becoming completely entangled in the taught lengths of paracord. One of the dangers when this happens is that the canopies are so close together, they can become entwined, or one of them can collapse. My parachute was slightly higher than the other, but both were still fully inflated with a little bit of separation, so my next concern was releasing the heavy rucksack attached to my front, because landing with that would risk breaking my legs. Looking below me, I saw the man I was entangled with was the T.A officer, who looked up at me worriedly.

"Don't worry if you can't lower your container." He said, thinking that it might fall on top of him. "You'll be alright if you land with it on."

"Yeah, that's not happening!" I muttered quietly to myself.

From exiting the aircraft to landing on the ground only takes about forty seconds with the LLP so there isn't much time for procrastination. I looked at the officer and knew there was a possibility that my kit could hit him and hurt him, but also knew that it could hurt me, plus, he was a STAB and an officer, and I didn't know him, so I dropped it anyway. Luckily, it dropped to the end of the suspension rope without striking him and dangled about a foot away from him as we descended. We landed close together in some nice and soft, marshy ground and collapsed our canopies quickly before removing our harnesses. Walking over to me, obviously hyped from the jump, the officer came over to talk. "What's your name?" he asked, extending his arm to shake hands. "I need to know it, for when I tell people about that entanglement. That was scary!"

"Private Brown Sir." I replied, briefly shaking hands. I didn't ask for his name, he was just a STAB (Stupid T.A Bastard)and I was too arrogant to care.

-PSYCHOTHERAPY-

RUNNING TO HELP
A FRIEND

When I learned about the death of my good friend Bryan Budd V.C in Afghanistan, I had only just returned there myself from paternity leave. It was the day after I returned, and I was sat in a large tent in Camp Bastion on my own, sheltering from the heat outside. Over a short period of time, I was informed by a few old friends from my old battalion, 3 Para, that Bry was missing after a firefight in Sangin, the most volatile town in Helmand Province. Later on, after a massive search and rescue mission had been conducted, I learned that he had died, and his body had been recovered from a field, close to a number of dead Taliban fighters that he had killed in his final moments.

My EMDR session started with me picturing that moment, where I was sat in the tent after being told he was missing. I could feel the pressure in my chest, and the crushing weight on my shoulders as I sat in the chair of the consultation room, worrying about Bry, dreading the worst. I was sat on a camp cot in civilian clothes and a pair of sandals.

"How does that make you feel, to know your friend Bryan is in trouble?" Dr Jackson asked.

"Anxious." I answered. "Anxious that he needs help. That he is alone."

"Stay with that thought, and think about what happens next, think about Bryan and how he feels and think about how you feel too." She suggested.

I pictured Bry. "He's lying on the ground. On his side." I said. "He knows his injuries are bad, but he's not flapping, he's calm. He knows the blokes are coming to help him."

I can still see that image now. Bry is lying on his right-hand side, looking straight at me. I described the scene. "He looks peaceful, in control, like he's deliberately remaining calm to keep his heart rate down."

"Hold that thought and think about what you are doing now, sat in that tent, waiting to hear about your friend Bryan?" the doctor asked.

I pictured myself standing up and exiting the tent, running towards the perimeter wall of the camp. "I'm running to help him." I Told her. In my mind's eye I watched from above, like video footage from a helicopter, and I could also see the 3 Para blokes getting into formation outside of the base, preparing to launch their rescue mission. They were already equipped and as desperate as I was to get to Bry, but the direct line I was embarking on was the shorter route. As I ran my clothing began to change from civilian to military and my pace steadily increased with every item change. My equipment loaded onto me next, and bits morphed onto my body like a character from the Power Rangers as I continued to accelerate. Body armour, helmet, webbing pouches and weapon attached onto me, and the more I got loaded up, the faster and more powerful I felt. By the time I got to the wall I was fully kitted out and a dust trail swirled behind me as I vaulted it in a giant leap. To my left I could hear 3 Para fighting their way through some fields and to my front and right the Taliban were shooting towards them. Without being able to see him, I could tell exactly where Bry was lying and continued sprinting without deviating from my trajectory, entering a field of high corn, and blasting through it until I exited into an open space where he lay on the ground. I was aware of two men sat on a hillside nearby and looked across to them hatefully. They were watching me as I stood over Bry's body and although they were not armed, I suspected that they had shot him.

As I described this fictional event to the doctor, which bore no geographical or factual resemblance to any real occurrence, I became more and more emotional. I knew that Bry was dying and no matter how fast we all worked to get to him, it seemed inevitable that we'd be too late.

"I want to fucking kill those c**ts!" I snarled angrily. That's not a word I use around women, so I was really upset.

The doctor prompted me once more. "When you think about that image of Bryan lying on the ground by the corn field, is there a word, or a feeling, or even an emotion that accompanies it?"

I let the image unfold naturally and looked at Bry's motionless body, realising that he was dead, and a wave of sadness added to the anger.

"He's dead." I stated glumly, refocusing on the two men on the hill as the tears ran down my nose and dripped onto the floor. My head was bowed forwards as I sat with my arms resting on my legs.

"And if you could say anything to Bryan in that moment, what would you say to him?" she asked.

I knew straight away, the words leapt out at me, but I delayed my answer because it was a strange one. In the image I placed my hand on Bry's shoulder.

"I love you mate." I said tearfully.

The next time I looked at the two men my anger had inexplicably subsided, and I was reluctant to admit it to my psychologist because it felt disloyal. I wanted to feel the rage, and I wanted the scene to develop further, to a point I where I was savagely exacting revenge on them, but it didn't. It came to a conclusion there. If time travel ever becomes a thing and I get to see Bry again I'll probably try to say something deep and meaningful but will end up with a mutual "Alright Airborne?" and a man hug.

-CHAPTER THREE-

RUN FOR YOUR LIFE

WRESTLERS ARE BADASSES

As a kid, up until the age of eight, there were only three television channels to choose from on English T.V; BBC 1, BBC 2, and ITV. On Saturdays ITV showed British wrestling, and the two biggest stars in the U.K were Big Daddy and Giant Haystacks. These two giants were household names and arch-rivals, Big Daddy being the "good guy" and Giant Haystacks the "baddy," and when they fought each other it was a massive event that drew millions of viewers. In the early 1990's I met Giant Haystacks once and the experience instilled in me a new-found respect for wrestlers and their potential to unleash real violence. The night I encountered him I was in Aylesbury town centre on my roller skates with a bunch of other skaters. We were heading for the Civic Centre multi-storey car park which had an excellent, smooth surface on the roof levels that were perfect for skating on. The car park was situated behind the Civic Centre which hosted lots of events such as live bands, comedians, pantomime, and wrestling. At the rear of the Civic Centre there was a fire exit that was reached by descending a wide flight of stairs, and on that door was a small sign that said, "Artistes Entrance." I think that the door doubled up as a semi-covert entry and exit point for the performers who wanted to leave the venue discretely, even though the overt sign com-promised its secrecy. When we got to the ground-level entrance to the car park one of the skaters noticed a woman with long, blonde hair, sitting in a car close to the exit. Being a teenage boy, with testosterone surging through his veins he wanted to see what she looked like and wolf-whistled, hoping that she would turn around, and we all stared to see if she'd respond. When she turned, we were disappointed to see what we considered at the time, to be an old woman, probably only 40 years old, but ancient to a bunch of teenagers. One of the boys also noticed a man sat next to her in the passenger seat.

"Is that Giant Haystacks!?" he shouted in surprise.

We all crouched to look into the car. It certainly looked like him. There was a big, bearded man, with long dark hair sitting the seat pushed all the way back but totally filling the space of the passenger side.

"It's Giant fucking Haystacks!" said another boy excitedly. "He was wrestling at The Civic earlier."

We moved closer to the car in curiosity. We'd all been brought up watching him on TV until the American WWF wrestling had taken over. One of the troublemakers didn't waste any time.

"You fat bastard! I hope you fucking lost!" he jeered loudly.

"Yeah, you fat fuck, wrestling is fake anyway you wanker!" shouted another boy.

The woman in the car wound down her window so Haystacks could shout across to us. "Fuck off you little c**ts!" he said angrily. "I'll come over there and smash your fucking heads in!"

We were surprised to hear him talk like that. He never swore on T.V and although he was a famous "baddie," we all knew it was just an act.

"Come on then fat boy. Come get us! Try not to have a heart attack chasing us though you fucking slob!"

The woman also shouted at us to defend Haystacks. "Go home before you get hurt boys!" she advised, unwittingly opening herself up for some abuse.

"Shut up you slag!" Came the sharp reply.

"Tell your slag to shut her fucking mouth!" shouted another boy. We were all winding each other up and getting carried away, but that last comment struck a nerve with Haystacks and his car door flung open and he got out. Whenever I remember the image of him standing up, it is accompanied by the sound they used to play when the Six Million Dollar Man (a 1970's

TV superhero) did something spectacular like jump really high or throw something colossal. He went up, and up, and up, and the suppressed suspension of the Ford Granada car seemed to breathe a sigh of relief as it returned to normal. He was huge! At 6ft 11 inches tall and weighing over 40 stones, to see him face to face was astonishing, the T.V couldn't prepare you for his physical stature. We all moved a few feet backwards in shock, bumping into one another as we did so, eyes fixated on the behemoth before us, gasping in awe. He was really angry now, it wasn't an act, he was furious. "When I get my hands on you, I'm going to fucking hurt you, you little shits!" he raged. He meant it too, and I believed him, he would have absolutely destroyed all of us. He was terrifying! However, one of the boys was still feeling brave. "Big Daddy can kick your arse, you old bastard!" he jibed once more.

Haystacks started running towards us, but none of us hung around to see how far he ran, we turned and legged it as fast as we could, not even looking back. After speed-skating a safe distance we stopped and laughed at each other nervously, we all knew how much danger we'd been in and we were buzzing. One of the lads suggested we go back and wind him up some more, but from a safer place, so we skated up to the first floor where we could lean over the wall and hurl more inappropriate, vile abuse at him and the lady in the car. They drove off as soon as we returned, he wasn't ever going to catch us, because we were far too cowardly to give him the opportunity.

Giant Haystacks 6'11"

Me at 5'7" with a few of the skater gang

BROOK WITH AN E AND
BROOK WITH AN EYE

Depot Para is a great place for young men to find a new career, especially those with psychotic tendencies, a high pain threshold and a sick sense of humour. Those who do not possess these attributes will either fail the course or acquire them during the brutal indoctrination process that is called recruit training. When we were taught about camouflage and concealment our instructors set up a little confirmation exercise at the end of the day to put all we had learnt into practice. At the bottom of a fern covered hill we were tasked to stealthily sneak our way up to the top and capture a lantern that was inside the back of a Land Rover. The instructors, 4 Corporals a Sergeant and a Captain would be patrolling the hill and if they saw us, would send us back to the bottom to start over again. At that point in training there were about forty recruits in the platoon, and we all scurried off in pairs to re-apply camouflage cream and stuff grass and moss into each other's clothing and equipment like we'd been taught, before the whistle blast initiated the exercise. We'd all spent hours the previous night sewing lengths of black elastic onto our equipment as a place to stuff the handfuls of grass, losing valuable hours of sleep because of our inept sewing skills.

When the whistle sounded, we began, crawling on our belt buckles as low to the ground and tactically as we could. I could hear the instructors calling out the names of people they'd seen and would then hear and see those people running down the hill to restart. I was about halfway up, moving very slowly and deliberately, inching my way through the undergrowth. As far as I could tell none of the instructors had seen me or were anywhere near me. Yeah right! The way I found out I was caught was when one of the Corporals whacked me on top of the head with a big stick. Even though I was wearing a helmet it rattled my brain and made my ears ring, stunning me for a couple of seconds before I reacted to the Corporals shouting.

"Brown you mong, you've been seen! Get away you horrible creature!"

I shook myself off, jumped up, sprinted down the hill and repeated that process for about an hour. Only one recruit made it into the Land Rover that night, Private Brook.

For the first couple of weeks our platoon had two Privates called Brook, and the way the instructors differentiated between them was by addressing one as "Brook" and the other as "Brook with an E" because that was how it was spelt. Neither of them passed Depot, one through lack of ability and one missed his family too much, so he left. Brook was a tall skinny bloke with a face only a mother could love and not the sharpest tool in the box. He was also overconfident in his camouflage and concealment abilities and when the Captain saw him and told him to go back to the start, Brook assumed it was Brook with an E that was compromised. The Captain we had was a short-tempered man who didn't like repeating himself.

"Brook!" he snapped again. "I can see you, get down the fucking hill!"

It gradually dawned on him that it might be him who was caught, and he slowly turned his head towards the angry officer to see that he was indeed looking straight at him.

"Double away you fucking mong!" The Captain screamed, unimpressed with the lethargic response as Brook slowly stood up and began walking away dejectedly.

Our Captain was known for his use of the blackboard eraser to wake up recruits who fell asleep during his class, he had thrown it accurately and effectively on several occasions but somehow, in that forest he had managed to find half a house brick instead. In his disproportionate rage, our Platoon Commander hurled that half-brick at Brook proving his accuracy with a foreign weapon was still exemplary when it smashed into his face splitting it wide open high on the cheekbone.

The officer examined the wound and knew it needed some medical treatment.

"Get yourself up to the top and find Corporal Rutledge, he'll clean you up." He said.

Cpl Rutledge took control of Brook and ushered him into the mobile, sterile, medical treatment facility a.k.a the back of the Land Rover, to carry out his assessment.

Part of the packing list for our kit was a sewing kit, called a "housewife."

"Take out your housewife." Instructed the stern-faced instructor.

Brook reached into his pouch and withdrew the small sewing kit and Cpl Rutledge threaded a length of black cotton through a needle and sewed the cut below Brooks' eye together. I know this because I saw Brook that evening and was shocked not only by the fact that his eye was swollen shut and his face was black and blue, but also by the horrendous stitches that had been performed on the wound. They looked like pieces of black cotton! He told me the story, and we both laughed about it. To us it only reinforced our belief that the Paras were awesome.

From then on, because of his swollen eye, Brook was renamed by the Corporals as "Brook with an Eye." Genius.

My Section learning camouflage and concealment
in the early days of recruit training

ANGRY ELEPHANTS

In 2000 I was on a training exercise in the Archers Post area of Kenya. We were working in six-man teams and marching through the night to a rendezvous (RV) point where we would commence live firing the following day. We had arrived in the country the previous day and part of the arrival process was to receive a briefing from a local landowner about the training area. He spoke about the environmental hazards of operating in the area which included the heat, flash floods, snakes, spiders and big game. According to his brief, at that time there was a rogue bull elephant in Archers Post that had been shot and wounded by a poacher. Its exact whereabouts were unknown, but he said it could well be in the area we were using. This revelation prompted a few questions from the audience on how we should deal with it if we came across it. The farmer explained that the elephant would be extremely angry and dangerous to humans and likely to attack if it saw or smelled us. I remember him explaining that it would be futile to try and hide behind foliage or climb trees because the elephant would simply smash through anything in its path to get to us. He said the best tactic was to get downwind of the elephant because it would primarily hunt us by scent. One soldier asked where to aim if we were to shoot at it, to achieve a kill shot. The farmer pointed out that the calibre of our rifles was a mere 5.56mm and it had already been shot by a .50cal hunting rifle (12.7mm) and we would probably just make it angrier. If we were to shoot though, he advised to aim for the front of the head at the centre point between the ear holes. Apparently, that is where the brain sits.

After a few hours marching across the arid ground of Archers

Post we stopped short of a river for the patrol commander to carry out a map check. He had chosen a crossing point from the map during his planning, but it was impossible to know if it was viable without physically checking. All of us were carrying a radio and wearing an earpiece so everyone knew what was happening when two of the team pushed forward towards the river to find a suitable crossing point. My earpiece crackled and one of the soldiers reported back to the patrol commander.

"John" he whispered. "We're fifty metres short of the river and it looks like there are some elephants at the crossing point."

There was a brief pause before he spoke again, this time with a slight sense of urgency. "There's definitely two elephants, and I think they've seen us." He said.

At the river, two elephants were at the water's edge enjoying a drink when they sensed the presence of the two men. The giant beasts turned to face them, only a short distance away, before one of them trumpeted out a loud warning. Everyone heard that unmistakeable sound, like the opening scene of a Tarzan film. The subsequent rapid thuds of their heavy flat feet pounding into the ground as they ran towards the two men was fairly distinct too. This time the voice on the radio was much more desperate and we could tell by the breathing and rustling noises that they were running.

"We're coming back to you! Prepare to move!"

The elephants had executed a mock charge, running towards the soldiers before stopping and letting out another angry trumpet blast, even louder than the first. The two men had turned to run as soon as the huge animals had moved towards them and before I knew it, they were sprinting past me, heading back the way we had come. The third, then fourth man shot past me too, beckoning me to follow, which I did in haste and the last man followed behind me as we all sprinted past him and continued running for about two hundred metres.

As the Patrol Commander studied the map to find an alternative crossing point one of the other teams arrived. They had chosen the same place to cross as us but after a quick update on the elephants also decided to find somewhere else, both parties agreeing to let the other know over the radio if they had success. Heading off in opposite directions we said our farewells and we moved down-river, keeping away from the water's edge. We had hardly got going when it happened again, this time without even a warning. One at a time the four men in front of me came backtracking past at full speed and guessing it was the elephants I sharply about turned and followed them. A familiar voice came on the radio as we were running, it was Al, the other patrol commander.

"John, I forgot to say, but we saw a hippo in the bush, in the area you're heading towards mate." He warned, a little late.

John replied, panting as he ran, but still chuckling. "Roger that mate, we've just met him! We're heading your way now!"

Apparently one of the blokes had almost bumped into it, he reckoned it was asleep standing up. Either way he was lucky, as hippos are extremely dangerous. After a bit of cautious searching, we all managed to cross the river safely and stayed as a group of twelve for a while until we got away from the dangers of the thirsty animals. Not long after getting across the water we heard two gunshots close by and headed towards the sound to investigate, discovering a third team of six, who had also just crossed the river. One of them had just shot a buffalo and killed it. Apparently, he had been walking through the bush when he heard a snort to his left and when he turned was face to face with a buffalo, only a few metres away. He said the beast had begun to charge towards him and he'd instinctively raised his rifle and fired two rounds at it, dropping it instantly. As he was explaining a 4x4 vehicle arrived, loaded up with men dressed in military clothing and carry rifles. They were Park Rangers who had heard the shots and come to check it wasn't poachers. When they saw the buffalo, they wanted to know how it had been killed and were shocked to learn it had been shot with an army issue rifle with such a small calibre. They were amazed that the soldier had killed it with only two rounds and not been killed himself. That was an eventful night that might sound fake, but it's true.

THROWN OUT OF THE PARTY

Every now and then a person joins a Battalion that everyone dislikes. It could be for numerous reasons, such as; they are lazy, unfit, selfish, untrustworthy, or cocky. One such bloke in 3 Para was a Private called Terry Johnson. He had come to Battalion directly from the Territorial Army (T.A), where he'd been a weekend warrior with 4 Para for a couple of years. Posted from the T.A meant he hadn't attended Depot, which already had peoples backs up, but his cocky attitude was what let him down. In 1999 he deployed to Kosovo with about half of 3 Para on peacekeeping operations and returned a couple of months later a self-proclaimed "war hero." The wife of a good friend of mine was working out in a gym in town when he walked in and shouted, "Hi ladies, it's okay, everyone calm down, the war hero is back!" His propensity to tell tales of his experiences in the Balkans soon earned him the nickname "Tetovo Terry," which was not geographically accurate, seeing as Tetovo is in North Macedonia, but it was close enough, and funny. One alcohol fuelled night in the accommodation, a load of blokes were getting ready to go into town when Tetovo Terry started boasting about what he'd done in Kosovo. Having been there themselves and knowing exactly what he had actually done, some of them quickly ran out of patience, and told him to leave before he got himself thrown out of the window. The accommodation block that he lived in was on a slope, and the back of the building where they were drinking was a fair bit higher from the ground than the front. Where they were, on the 3rd floor was basically four floors up from the ground at the rear. The eternal antagonist, Terry goaded the others on, saying how he'd like to see them try etc. etc, and tired of listening to his nonsense a couple of the blokes grabbed hold of him and as promised, threw him out of the window. Despite his attempts to resist, they forced him out through the small space, slapping at his hands and feet as he tried to wedge them in the frame, and after a small struggle he ended up hanging on to the window frame by his fingers. The blokes weren't trying to kill him, just scare him a bit to shut him up, but as he hanged there dangling from the window, someone with a low IQ, and even lower tolerance for Terry walked into the room. Instead of rushing to help him, he ran over and bashed Terry's fingers with his fist, forcing him to let go of the window frame and fall. Luckily, as he plummeted, he somehow managed to athletically grab hold of the window below on the 2nd floor and heaved himself up and into someone else's room. No doubt he bored whoever was in there too. Those guys! Such pranksters!

IN THE GHETTO

In 2012, after a few weeks of running survival training in the Belizean jungle, I managed to get a few days off in Miami. I was going there on my own, to do some mixed martial arts (MMA) training, and my wife searched the internet for me back home to find some cheap accommodation. I arrived at a hostel on South Beach in the evening and at first, I had the room, with two bunk beds to myself. I'd found the addresses of several gyms and my plan was to explore them all and choose the best one, so when I saw a Bike Hire shop close to the hostel while out for a walk, I decided to check out their prices in the morning. The guy in the shop was an ex- U.S Marine, a massive, muscular bloke who also trained MMA and he advised me to get an electric bike when I told him where I planned on going. We got on well straight away and he offered me the electric bike at the same price as a manual one, but I wasn't having any of that. "You Marines might need a battery to power your bikes." I joked. "But I'm a Paratrooper, I've got these bad boys!" I said cockily, pointing to my legs.

He laughed. "Okay man, but if you change your mind, come back and I'll sort you out."

The bike I got was a single-speed cruiser with a shopping basket over the back wheel and "Hire Me" stickers plastered all over the frame. That day I cycled around the whole of Miami, getting flyers and timetables from every club I could find, covering about forty miles. At one point as I cycled down a street, I noticed a sign and recognised the name of the area "Little Haiti" as one of the districts my Lonely Planet travel guidebook recommended to avoid because of the high crime rate and the more I looked, the more I realised that it did indeed look pretty rough. Not only that, but I stood out like a sore thumb too. As a white man, in shorts and flip-flops, riding a shopping bike, with a basket and "Hire Me" all over it, I was quite easy to pick out as a tourist, and despite my efforts to pick up my speed, the never-ending intersections and traffic lights hindered progress. At one set of lights a police officer was standing next to his patrol vehicle, so I dismounted and approached him for a bit of reassurance. "Excuse me sir." I said politely. "Could you tell me the best way to find this gym please?" I showed him the flyer and he gave me directions to the MMA gym, which I already knew. We engaged in some small talk when he picked up on my accent, before I asked him my real question. "Is this a good area? Is it okay around here?" I asked casually, trying not to show my apprehension.

"That depends on what do you mean by okay?" he replied cryptically.

Using my finger, I pointed to the ground and moved it in a large circular motion as I said. "Is it safe round here?"

"Hell no!" he chuckled. "It's not safe! You'll get plenty of MMA practice around here!"

I thanked him and got back on my bike, only getting a few feet before he called me back. In my mind I thought he was going to tell me to get in his vehicle and give me a lift out of there for my safety.

"I just remembered, there's a quicker way to that gym." he said before giving me new directions and sending me on my way again. When I got to the gym I dismounted and leant the bike against the wall next to the entrance. I'd taken about two steps when someone shouted out, "If you leave that bike there, it won't be there when you come out!" I looked up to see a man leaning out of a window above me, smoking a cigarette.

"Is it ok to take it inside?" I asked.

"Hell yeah, you better, if you wanna keep it!" he answered.

I'd already made my mind up that I wasn't going to train there but went inside for a look anyway. The gym looked great, with loads of blokes doing hard sparring in a fenced off matted area, and the prices were good too, but getting there and back, especially in the night-time would be far too risky. I got back on my bike and headed back towards South Beach, passing through another recommended no-go area called Wynwood on my way. Finally arriving back at South Beach after a long day, I rode straight to the Cycle Hire shop, cap in hand, to eat a huge slice of humble pie.

"I'll take that electric bike!" I said, to the owners amusement.

I used that bike every day to get to the gym I chose which was about twelve miles from the hostel and as much as didn't want to admit it, it was awesome. It had a top speed of eighteen miles per hour, the acceleration from a static start was fantastic and the battery charge lasted all day. The only time it was a problem, was when I wanted to go faster than eighteen miles per hour, which happened a couple of times in dodgy areas, late at night. It seemed like the bike was limited to the top speed and no matter how hard I pedalled, it wouldn't go any faster.

-PSYCHOTHERAPY-

PEACE IN THE FOREST

The forest has always been a good place for me to relax and find peace and quiet. It's also my favourite place to run, cycle and walk my dog. Whenever I move to a new house, I purchase an Ordnance Survey map of the local area to find nearby woods and forests to explore. I love the way you can immerse yourself in the environment and enjoy the flora and fauna while at the same time find protection from the environment such as the wind, rain, and man-made mechanical and technological distractions. For one year of my childhood from around the ages eight to nine years old I lived on a council estate in Surrey, on the edge of a large forest. All the kids spent hours playing in those woods, building camps, climbing trees, and exploring every track and trail. Everyone carried a knife, not for bravado or violence but as a tool for sharpening sticks as spears or arrows and carving their initials into the bark of trees. As an adult, I spent a fair amount of time in forests too, a lot of it in the military where it was generally unpleasant and usually included being cold and wet, or in the jungle where it is hot and wet. After becoming a survival instructor, I learned to appreciate the forest much more as I was able to identify the resources it provides for shelter, first aid, fire, navigation, water, and food. Every time I visit a forest, usually accompanied by my Golden Retriever, Barney, I try to learn something new or at least revise knowledge I already have.

When undergoing EMDR therapy I would go into a trance-like state where I was fully immersed in my thoughts, like how I imagine hypnotherapy feels. When told that I would be trying EMDR therapy I deliberately resisted the urge to research it as I wanted to go into it open minded, without any preconceptions on how it worked or how I should respond. These sessions were often very intense and could affect me for hours or days afterwards. During one of my EMDR sessions with Dr Jackson she asked me to imagine a place where I could find happiness and calm. The first place I thought of was a forest in Cornwall called Wilsey Down, where we used to train and assess new survival instructors. I pictured myself on a dirt track that runs through the woods and settled in for the session, not knowing where it would lead, or if there was even an intended objective by the doctor. As cliché as it sounds, without influence I experienced something I was not expecting at all. As the session progressed, I found myself in a small grassy opening in the woods, surrounded by a mixture of small coniferous and deciduous trees which stood about 20 feet high. If the aim of the session were to help me feel peaceful, it had worked. I could feel and describe in detail the ground beneath my feet, the temperature and flow of the air and the sounds of the singing birds and rustling branches. As we spoke my point of view changed from first-person to observer and I watched myself through a rotating lens that slowly circled my body like a drone camera. Gradually I became lighter and lighter, as if a huge weight were being lifted from my shoulders and my posture changed in response, standing up tall, shoulders drawing back and head lifting to an upright position. A feeling of euphoria swept over me as I began to rise from the ground and my head lifted to face the sky. My arms opened out from my sides, palms facing upwards as I continued to watch myself from ground level, still circling through 360 degrees. In that moment I felt truly happy, free from anger, anxiety, and worry. I was verbalising my feelings to the doctor, enjoying the experience of what it feels like to be stress free for a moment when I suddenly realised what I was witnessing.

"I've just realised what is happening." I said to the psychologist solemnly. "It's my death, I'm dead!"

I think she was as surprised as I was, and I highly doubt it was the intended outcome of the session, it was probably the opposite, but that was what I was envisioning. At that time, I was having suicidal thoughts every day but that was the first time I had envisaged it in detail like that. It almost reinforced my irrational thoughts that suicide would bring me comfort or happiness. The irony was not lost on me in that consultation room, I was supposed to be working towards wellness but sometimes it seemed unachievable. There were a few times like that during my treatment where I found myself in the paradoxical situation where I felt sympathy for my doctor and wanted to reassure her that she had done nothing wrong. It must have been disheartening when a session that seemed to be going really well got flipped on its head into such a negative conclusion.

-CHAPTER FOUR-

IT'S A JUNGLE OUT THERE

OPERATION CERTAIN DEATH

In 2000 me and a few of the blokes were in the barrack block looking forward to a night of drinking and partying in Stowmarket, the local town to our camp at Wattisham Airfield. It was Friday afternoon and as always, we had finished early for the weekend. There was a telephone on the wall in the corridor that was seldom used but it rang that day. A message was passed on that nobody was to go home or travel more than 4 hours away because something was happening. Shortly afterwards there came another call, this time we were instructed to stay within 30 minutes of camp. Soon a third call ordered everyone back to the compound for a briefing. We all hastily made our way back to our HQ which was located at the arse end of camp, away from everyone else where we could keep out of trouble. I had never heard of Sierra Leone before, but it was kicking off there and the UK government wanted boots on the ground to facilitate a non-combatant evacuation (NEO) operation. We had a quick intelligence brief from one of the officers, loaded up the vehicles and weapons and prepared our personal kit for the African bush / jungle environment. On Sunday we were debussing from a helicopter onto the airport tarmac in Freetown, Sierra Leone fully loaded up with rifles, machine guns, hand grenades and anti-tank rockets. Not long after we got there, we were given orders to deploy to a small village where the enemy force was expected to pass through on their way to attack Freetown. Details were vague but there were estimated to be between 600 and 2000 psychotic men and boy soldiers from the Revolutionary United Front (RUF) advancing to Freetown, leaving a trail of murder, mutilation, rape and kidnapping in their wake. Our orders were not the most inspiring and the way I remember it we were told to hold the village for as long as possible and if overrun, withdraw through the jungle, making our way back to Freetown. "Dead or alive, no one gets left behind!" were words actually uttered, and I genuinely thought we were going to take a lot of casualties. I know it has probably been used on every operation since time began but after our abysmal orders, some of the blokes jokingly nicknamed it "Operation Certain Death."

Inserting to the village on board another helicopter I remember sitting with my rifle between my legs, barrel pointing down, looking around at the other soldiers. Nobody really talks in military aircraft because they are so noisy, so everyone was taking the time to reflect or contemplate the coming days. I was single at the time and when I thought about the impact my death would have on others, I knew that my mum would be the hardest hit, she would be devastated, but apart from her there would be no massive effect. As I looked at the other paratroopers, I assessed their worthiness of survival against mine one by one. Some were married or had girlfriends, some I knew, had children and I honestly thought that because of that their lives were more important than mine, in a just world I would be killed before them. Those like me, young, single men sat at the bottom of my scale of importance, but I was no more worthy than anyone. I never told the blokes about that, but I never forgot it, it taught me a lot about myself. In later years on other tours, I would become one of those with a girlfriend, then a wife, then a child, but I still never made it up the ladder, I think I just settled at the bottom along with everyone else.

As well as us, there was a platoon of Nigerian soldiers at the village and we split the perimeter defence responsibilities in half, with us taking the 180 degrees toward the likely enemy threat and the Nigerians at the rear. The villagers were friendly enough and left us alone and the Nigerians were a good bunch, at least they were to us anyway. The two nearest to my position were called Sunday and Mohammed and they were a little bit crazy. Sunday told me that the rebels were so afraid of the Nigerians that if they ever captured or killed one of them, they killed them twice, the second time with a six-inch nail driven into their head, through the eye. The rebels were scared they would get up and come after them if they didn't. The Nigerians had been peacekeeping in Sierra Leone for a while and were very strict with the population, beating them with sticks if ever they felt they had been disrespected. The first time I witnessed this was when a local man rode past Mohammed on his bicycle. The usual protocol was for them to dismount and walk past the soldiers, only getting back on their bikes when a suitable distance away. One of my mates, Ginge, who was always winding people up didn't miss this opportunity and called out to Mohammed.

"Mohammed, he's taking the piss out of you!" He shouted, pointing to the man on the bike. "Are you going to let him get away with that?" Ginge was a wind-up merchant but he wasn't nasty and didn't expect the reaction he got.

Mohammed jumped up and chased after the cyclist, long stick in hand, shouting angrily. The young man stopped and stood still, holding his bike upright between his legs. As he made his last couple of paces Mohammed raised his stick in the air and brought it down quickly, hitting the shoulder of his target who fell off the bike sideways and defended himself by curling up in the foetal position on the ground and pleading for mercy. Mohammed struck him several more times while loudly berating his insolence, before calmly walking back to his post like he'd just popped to the neighbours to borrow some sugar.

Woken from my sleep by screaming and shouting one morning I sat up quickly on the patch of dirt that was my bed. The screams were coming from a small clearing on the edge of the village in between my position and the position where Sunday and Mohammed lived. I got up and walked towards the noise.

After a few steps I could see what all the fuss was about. A group of about six boys around 10-14 years old were lined up on the ground face down, balancing on just their foreheads and tip toes, with their hands behind their backs and asses in the air. Sunday and Mohammed were walking around and between the boys whipping them violently with long sticks that they had cut down from a tree branch, shouting the whole time. The boys were crying, and their bodies shook from holding the stressful position, but the soldiers showed no empathy. I had no idea what had occurred prior to this but it was clearly not ethical or within their jurisdiction, however I did not intervene, instead returned to my piece of dirt to get a brew on. Africa can be a harsh, violent place where brutality is an accepted reality and sometimes you just have to keep your nose out of other people's business. Later that day I asked Sunday why he had beaten the boys.

"They are rebels!" He said emphatically.

"Who are rebels?" I asked.

Sunday gestured towards the village with a sweeping motion of his hand. "All of them!" He was a little bit unhinged.

During the first couple of days at the village we received a warning from HQ that the rebels were close and to prepare for their imminent attack. Our Sergeant Major negotiated with the village elders and got the locals to dig trenches all around the perimeter for us to use to defend it. They grafted and did a fantastic job, saving us hours of work. He also asked them to clear the trees and foliage around the village so that we had clear arcs of view and fire and the enemy would be denied them to cover their approach. Some of us went on a patrol for a couple of hours and when we came back, I was gobsmacked by the amount of work the locals had done. Chopping down and burning back the forest, they had somehow cleared a massive area already and the fires were still burning. I didn't think they would be able to stop the fires.

"How far back are you going?" One of the blokes asked a worker.

"Until you say stop." He replied.

The Sergeant Major told them to stop, and they used their skills to put the fires out quickly. We were ready.

There was no attack that night. We manned the trenches, taking turns to keep watch through our night sights, watching, listening, and waiting for the rebels to launch their attack. I was so tired I was hallucinating. I remember seeing a man kneeling with a rifle in one hand and staring at him, waiting for him to move. The image didn't make sense because it looked like someone wearing WW2 clothing and holding an old Lee Enfield .303 rifle. I put the night sight down, shook my head then re-acquired the view. Surprisingly, I could still see it, like when you see a face in a stain on the ceiling, I couldn't un-see it, but I knew it wasn't real. I had experienced this several times before after sleep deprivation and when dawn broke, I realised it was just a tree stump in the distance. The attack would come a couple of days later.

Pathfinder Platoon in Lungi Loi 2000

The night of the attack I had just taken post in the sentry position and stood in the trench with the General-Purpose Machine Gun (GPMG) resting on its bipod on the ground. The bloke I had taken over from was Loz and he was sorting himself out before going back to sleep. I heard someone approach from behind and turned to see Sunday approach in a half squat. Kneeling next to my trench he whispered to me "They are here, get ready!"

"Who is here mate?" I asked.

"The rebels!" he said adamantly, pointing into the darkness.

I picked up the night scope and scanned the area to my front. "Well, I can't see anybody." I stated dismissively. The Nigerians didn't even have night vision equipment so I doubted he could see better than me.

"They are here!" repeated Sunday, and he turned around and ran back to his position.

Immediately after he left a message came over the radio that I had never heard before so I called out to Loz as quietly as I could.

"Loz!" I said. "They just called Maximise on the net. I guess that means stand-to?"

"Yes it does mate." Loz answered immediately.

"Get everyone up mate!" I ordered. "Stand-to, stand-to!"

Standing-to is to prepare for an attack, to be at red alert / battle stations etc. and all the blokes were up and in the trenches with their weapons in the shoulder within seconds.

The rebels were indeed here, just like Sunday had warned and they were using the main dirt road as their approach route. Back then we weren't equipped all that well with technology and our machine guns didn't have mounts to attach night sights. The two soldiers manning the trench next to the road waited patiently as the rebels silently walked towards them. Paul manned the machine gun, while Mick held the night vision scope to his eye, describing what he was observing to the gunner quietly. Paul was an excellent soldier from 1 Para and like me had only been in the Pathfinders for about six months. We had met on the first day of our Pathfinder selection course and quickly became good friends. He was extremely keen and a consummate professional with a passion for innovation and development. Unfortunately, there were a couple of "old sweats" who resented this, preferring the notion that "new guys" should be seen and not heard and would always try to shoot him down and undermine his proposals. Paul and Mick never really got the credit for their actions that night, but they were outstanding. When the rebels, who had still not been positively identified at this point, got close, a Nigerian soldier called out to the first shadowy figure to halt and identify himself. At that point the rebels opened fire with their AK47's sending a volley of bullets towards the village, the tracer rounds streaking across the sky like angry fireflies. Paul returned fire with the GPMG, doing his best to aim it where he saw the muzzle flash, firing a short, controlled burst of the 7.62mm ammunition. Mick, resisting the natural instinct to take cover, stood tall and observed where Paul's shots landed and gave him corrections.

"Right a bit!" He said clearly.

Paul fired again.

"Up a bit!" Mick directed, seeing the rounds strike the ground in front of the target.

Paul adjusted and fired another short burst which missed by a fraction but was good enough.

"On!" Confirmed Mick.

Paul held his aim and fired multiple bursts, this time hitting the rebel who was also firing back at him, killing him where he stood.

"He's down!" Said Mick. "Switch right one fist." He immediately started to direct him on to the next target and did the same until he was also neutralised, then continued that process. To work as a pair like that took tremendous discipline from both men. I think alot of people wouldn't be able to do that and would end up firing recklessly and inaccurately instead. They weren't the only ones firing of course, several of the other PF blokes also engaged, successfully repelling the attack but I think the initial fire laid down, and damage done by those two is what put the shits up the rebels, ultimately making them turn and flee back into the jungle.

Later that morning we were reinforced by a platoon from 1

Para, who took over our positions so that we could conduct a follow-up patrol to try and catch the retreating enemy. The Nigerians had already been out in one of their vehicles and driven down the road for a few hundred metres, returning with a dead body unceremoniously draped over the bonnet. On the road there were more bodies and I remember how one of them was laid down on his back with one arm raised in the air. It looked like he was shielding the sun from his eyes, but the glare of the sun was the least of his worries, he was extremely dead. Our Platoon Sergeant, Steve Heaney M.C took command of the patrol and we headed through the jungle, handrailing the track, towards the next village which was about 2km away. As we walked, we saw plenty of evidence that the rebels had been there. There were blood trails, expended ammunition cases, weapons, including a Rocket Propelled Grenade (RPG) and several items of clothing including a cowboy hat and some flip flops. When we arrived at the outskirts of the next village Steve quickly organised us into fire support and assault teams and dispatched us methodically to clear the mud-hut buildings under his tight control. The way he adapted to the situation and organised us was impressive, he was an excellent soldier with an outstanding reputation for his abilities, but he was also a ruthless commander that you didn't want to get on the wrong side of. It was something we had never trained for or rehearsed but we went through that village, clearing every building like a well-oiled machine. Unfortunately, the rebels had scarpered although there was evidence to show we had only just missed them. We moved further into the jungle quickly, using the indigenous trails for best speed, but after a while Steve called a halt to the mission and we made our way back to our own village. We were later told that the rebels had buried another nine of their men in that village, but we never went back there.

The next time I saw Sunday I asked him. "How did you know the rebels were coming last night?"

He replied sincerely. "I heard them!" he said.

He was further away from them than I was, and he had no radio communications, so I didn't believe him.

"Seriously, how did you know?" I repeated my question.

"I heard them coming!" he stated firmly and walked off.

Me in a news article while we were in Sierra Leone

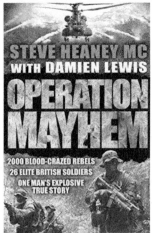

Book by Sgt Steve Heaney M.C about Operation Palliser, Sierra Leone

SNAKES ARE NASTY BASTARDS

In 1996 I was on a course in the Brunei jungle called the Long-Range Reconnaissance Patrol course. One day we were down at the river washing ourselves and our clothing of all the dirt and sweat after a hard day's graft, when I discovered three baby Coral Snakes underneath a rock. I stepped back and called out to the others to alert them so that they would not accidentally stumble across the snakes. They weren't bothering us, so I thought it best to just leave them in peace and keep away. A Gurkha from another team walked over to me and asked to see them and we both crouched down to observe them. As quick as a flash, without batting an eyelid, the Gurkha withdrew his Kukri knife from the sheath on his belt and diced them up like a chef chopping carrots.

"You jack bastard!" I snapped, completely surprised by his actions. "What did you do that for?" The snakes were no threat to us.

"Bloody snakes innit." He replied with a grin. He seemed relieved. "Bloody bastards' mate!" He said before re-sheathing his blade and walking away. I was a bit gutted, they were the first baby snakes I'd ever seen.

Another day, early in the morning we were walking along the jungle track to the teaching area when a Bruneian soldier suddenly stopped. He raised his hand to signal to us to stop, which we did, and I asked another of the Bruneians what was the matter. He told me that they had spotted a snake. The first Bruneian withdrew his machete, stepped off the path and cut down a branch from a tree, quickly removing the smaller branches and twigs so that within seconds it was fashioned into a pole, about 8 feet long. The snake was right in the middle of the well-trodden pathway and was standing up on its tail aggressively hissing. Gripping one end of the pole the young soldier raised it high above his head before bringing it down in a fast, chopping motion to strike the snake hard. The snake dropped flat on the ground motionless, and the man rapidly hit it two or three more times before using the pole to fling it into the trees. That was the first wild snake I ever saw. That scenario took seconds, he had obviously done that before, and they explained that the snake was very territorial, aggressive, and deadly venomous before carrying on to the first lesson of the day. At that time, if I had spotted the snake, I would probably have just walked around it, giving it a wide berth, but it was their country and that was clearly how they dealt with snakes.

In the Belizean jungle, the locals act similarly. One time I was sat by a fire having a brew with a couple of locally employed civilians when a snake decided to take a short cut through our small clearing. I hadn't even noticed it, but they had, and without even a pause in conversation one of them casually picked up his machete, leaned over to the side and chopped off its head with an outstretched arm as it tried to slither past. If that had been a bunch of Brits people would have been out of their seats either running away or throwing things at it, but their relaxed response to the snake made me also feel at ease and I didn't react.   "Do you always kill the snakes you see?" I asked, genuinely wanting to learn. They both nodded and the guy who'd used the machete spoke.

"Always!" he said sincerely. "If not, maybe someone will tread on it in the night, or maybe tomorrow it bites someone and it kills them. We always kill the snake."

In 2000 while we were deployed to Sierra Leone on Operation Palliser a British newspaper printed a story about us that read "Snail soup and Cobra Casserole." A journalist had visited our location and learned that we had been supplementing our rations with some of the local wildlife that the locals had provided. Some of the blokes had eaten snake, giant snails, and chickens from a nearby jungle village.

Newspaper article from May 2000. At the front is Ginge and behind him Paul, who directed the machine gun fire onto target when we were attacked in Sierra Leone

Walking into my mother-in-law's house during a visit one time, I noticed a rather unpleasant smell which turned out to be coming from a terrarium in the hallway. My brother-in-law had gone on holiday and asked her to look after his Corn Snake called Doris. My wife mentioned the smell to her, and she admitted that the glass habitat had not been cleaned out for about a week. She was too scared put her hands in the terrarium and asked if we'd clean it for her. Fair enough I thought, lots of people have a phobia of snakes.

"You're okay with snakes aren't you Steve?" she asked.

I'm no hero by any stretch, but I'm alright with most animals as long as the owner says they're safe. "No more than anyone else, but yeah I don't mind them." I replied, knowing that I was volunteering myself.

"Can you clean out the cabinet for me then please? I'm too scared!" she said.

I'd never done it before so I asked her what was required, and she explained how the snake would need picking up and transferring to another container while the cabinet was cleaned out, then popping back in.

"Is that alright?" she asked.

It seemed straight forward enough, and it was only a pet. "Yes, I can do that Pam." I answered. "As long as it doesn't bite." I said casually, assuming that was an obvious condition.

"Oh, she bites alright! She's a nasty bugger!" My mother-in-law exclaimed.

"What do you mean?" I queried. "She always bites? Or sometimes bites, if you handle her wrong?"

"No, she always bites as soon as you go anywhere near her! That's why I won't clean it." She replied.

"Then sorry, but I'm not doing it either!" I said.

I might be mad, but I ain't stoopid!

As a military survival instructor, I went to the USA to conduct desert survival training several times. One of the places we used regularly was the Mojave Desert in Nevada which is home to one of the deadliest snakes in America, the Mojave Green Rattlesnake. This snake has a fearsome reputation and is often described as extremely aggressive toward humans, with a bite that will probably kill you if not treated with antivenom quickly. During one course in 2010 I was on the training area talking to a local Park Ranger called Jonathan that we had befriended and done some instructor training with. He was very knowledgeable and passionate about the desert and had driven out to visit our course. While we were talking there was a bit of commotion in the staff bivouac area and one of the blokes told me that there was a rattle snake next to someone's shelter, and they were trying to shoo it away without hurting it. Jonathan and I headed over to have a look and I picked up a long-handled shovel from the back of a vehicle as I walked past it. Sure enough, there was a rattler coiled in the shade of a Creosote Bush, rattling his tail to deter us from encroaching any further. Including our students there were about forty people in that area, most of whom were sleeping on the floor that night. I looked at Jonathan and asked him. "What would *you* do with that rattler?" I asked.

"What do *you* want to do with it?" he replied.

I wasn't sure about the legalities or conservation rules, and he was a Ranger, so I wasn't too sure how to answer, but the safety of the course was my priority, so I answered honestly.

"I want to fucking kill it!" I said at the risk of offending him.

"I'd kill it." He responded bluntly.

"Roger that." I said. We both knew that I was seeking permission and we both knew it was the sensible thing to do to protect everyone. Nestled under the Creosote Bush there was no way I could get a clear shot so one of the blokes used a stick to beat the ground and usher the snake to move. As it emerged from the bush in a dash towards the next bush, I used the shovel to decapitate it, cutting a few inches further back from the head than intended, but achieving a clean cut with the first strike. The snake twisted and contorted a little then lay still. Using the shovel again I picked up the body and we used it to practice skinning and gutting with one of the blokes keeping the skin for himself. A short while later I dug a hole to bury the snake head to ensure no one accidentally stood on its fangs and got envenomated. It had been 5 or 10 minutes since I'd despatched it, but I still used the shovel to pick it up, and when the edge of the shovel touched the rattler it struck. Its teeth made an audible "ding" as they bit at the metal, the few inches of neck flexing quickly as it defended itself. That thing looked like pure evil attacking the shovel blade. I couldn't believe it was still alive! I gave it another whack, this time with the flat side of the shovel then scooped it up and tipped it into the hole before back filling it with sand.

Don't mess with snakes, they are nasty bastards!

BORNEO BOB

It's probably just the same in certain civilian trades, but in the army, there is a tendency for people to believe that everything must have been harder in the old days. Encouraging and enforcing this notion in every unit are a handful of self-proclaimed "Old Sweats" who also view themselves as some kind of unofficial regimental historians and spokesmen for values and standards. In my experience these people are usually fat, lazy, bitter, thirty-something year old men with a very blurred memory of who they are and what they've done, and they always claim to have been dealt a bad hand, which accounts for why they've stagnated, while others in their peer group have excelled. I remember plenty of hard times in my career but when I was in Depot, going through recruit training we were told that Depot used to be much harder. As a crow in Battalion, we apparently had it easy compared to the old days, where you got beat up all the time and had to sleep outside. Equipment used to be heavier, load carries were faster, with more weight, the old issue rifle was better, and everyone always did a 10 miler on Friday mornings (quicker and heavier than us.) I used to wonder how fucking hard it must have been in the 1940's seeing as though it had apparently gotten easier at every turn of the wheel. After serving nearly 27 years in the army I can honestly say that I have never seen this theory proven to be correct, and even if it was, the young soldiers have no control over it anyway, all they can do is what's put in front of them. During my service I did a lot of fitness training and most of my close friends were extremely fit, we trained at least twice a day, even at weekends, but even we didn't do the amount of "airborne ten-milers" that the big-time bluffers claimed to have done. Para Battalions are full of excellent soldiers who are extremely fit, motivated, and capable, but sometimes defenceless youngsters are force fed bullshit and their achievements undermined by a minority of insecure has-beens. The number of times I've heard people who I've never seen in the gym or out running, tell a young soldier about how they used to do a ten-miler every single Friday for years and years is embarrassing.

When I was a Private in 3 Para Signals Platoon, we had a Lance Corporal like that, and he set the standard the first time I spoke to him. His name was Bob, and he was talking about the "Old Sigs" which I was obviously too new to know anything about because I had only just been posted into the Sigs Platoon.
"In the old Sigs, they called me Borneo Bob." He said in between puffs on a rolled-up cigarette.
I already knew about the Jungle Training Centre in Brunei, which is part of the island of Borneo, and wanted to go there.
"Have you been to Brunei?" I asked, keen to know more.
"No." he replied bluntly, shaking his head.
"So why did they call you Borneo Bob?" I said, trying to piece it together.
"Because last year I spent six weeks in Kathendini!" he stated boastfully.
"Kathendini? As in the Kathendini jungle in Kenya?" I queried.
"Yep. I did six weeks straight in the trees. The only person to do it." He stated proudly.

Bob had a lot of good stories that were probably loosely based on actual events from his, or plagiarised from someone else's past, but even those that were clearly fake were worth listening to. The best ones were delivered under the influence of alcohol and we'd gather around to hear them, deliberately ignoring obvious flaws and contradictions to allow the tale to flow. You knew it was going to be a good one when he started with his favourite scene-setter.
"There I was, Para Regt-shirt, cut-off jeans, desert boots, all-day-

session."

At that point we'd exchange knowing glances with each other, eyes widening, eyebrows raising and mouth edges curling upwards in suppressed smiles of anticipation.

When I joined 3 Para in 1994 just about everyone did dress like that. We were sold our desert boots by our Depot staff at an inflated price and the more battered, beer and bloodstained they were, the better. Clean desert boots were a clear sign that the wearer was not a hardened drinker and might as well be painted fluorescent yellow with the words "Joe" on the left and "Crow" on the right. A new pair would be deliberately dirtied-up by walking through puddles and scuffing them on everything in sight the first time they were worn. Blue jeans and maroon regimental t-shirts were worn by the entire 5 Airborne Brigade, but it was easy to distinguish an individual's parent unit by the cap badge emblazoned on the left breast. I loved it when it was like that because it was like being in a massive gang and easy to identify friend from foe. During Leave you would often see a bloke out running or walking through the street with a maroon top and strike up conversation. At one point I remember counting the tops in my locker and I had thirteen regimental and battalion tops, with only one plain civvy one.

Bob continued to set the scene, not only was he on an all-day drinking binge, but he was also wearing a huge plaster-cast on his leg, from foot to groin. Why? Because he'd broken his leg in a parachuting accident of course! Anyway, while he was sat down with his crutches by his side, a big man walks into the pub with a beautiful girl on his arm and looks straight at Baz, sneering at his Para Reg attire.

"Cracking t-shirt mate!" he said sarcastically.

Bob noticed that the antagonist was also wearing a military t-shirt, a green one with another cap badge on it and the words "Falkland Islands 1983" scribed below it. Knowing full well that the Falklands War was in 1982 Bob retorted quickly, pointing at the man's top and snorting. "Says you! What were you doing, picking up the fucking brass!?" (Brass is the empty casing left behind from an expended ammunition round.)

Apparently, the man replied with an old favourite of the anti-para fraternity.

"Only two things fall out of the sky." He quipped. "Bird shit, and paratroopers!"

At this point, Borneo Bob stood up, grabbed one of his crutches and said. "Yeah, and they both make a mess of your head!" Proceeding to smash it over the top of the bloke's head before beating the living piss out of him on the floor. Then after downing the rest of his pint he collected his other crutch and left the pub with the unconscious bloke's goddess girlfriend in tow, totally seduced by Bob's fighting prowess.

We had no idea how much, if any of that story was real but we didn't care, because it was awesome!

PADDLING WITH CROCODILES

One of my trips to Belize was to attend the International Long Range Reconnaissance Course (ILRRP) in 2001. I'd already completed the jungle LRRP course in Brunei in 1996 and that was one of the hardest things I've ever done, so I knew it would be arduous. This time it was much more enjoyable though because I was the Patrol Commander and able to manage the team my own way, and we all got on well. Also on the course were some Dutch Marines, Dutch Army, Belizean Defence Force and Ukrainian Army teams. The Ukrainian soldiers were quite aloof and kept to themselves, probably due to the language barrier, but were polite and engaging if you made the effort. Their Patrol Commander was a huge man who wore a horizontally striped blue and white t-shirt, like that worn by the Soviet Union Spetsnaz under his shirt. He was easily the oldest man on the course and looked like he'd been through the wringer. Not muscular and not thin, he was just big, and he had the appearance of an old-school hard nut, that could hang you upside down in a dark basement, electrocute you by the testicles with a car battery, pull your teeth out with a rusty set of pliers, then go home and tell his wife he'd had a boring day at the office. He told me that he'd been in the Soviet Special Forces before the Ukraine gained its independence, where his job was to infiltrate foreign countries and carry out assassinations on key political personnel. For all I know, he was a chef, but he was convincing enough. At the end of the course all of the students congregated at a place called Guacamayo Bridge, where we all sat down with our feet hanging over the engorged river to clean our rifles and get some sun on our pasty white bodies. A recent downpour had caused flash floods and the river was still subsiding, leaving a muddy pond on the riverbank at one end of the bridge. As we arrived, we were briefed by the instructors that there were three crocodiles in that pond, and we were not to enter the water.

The SA80 rifle we were all using, including the foreign soldiers, is a fiddly weapon when it comes to stripping and assembling and one of the things that can happen if you are not careful is the recoil rods and spring can eject from the weapon like a projectile. When this happens, it makes a very distinct sound, and as we sat on Guac Bridge, we heard it, immediately followed by the plopping sound of something falling into water. Everyone looked towards the sound and the Brits exclaimed, "OOhh!" Someone had just lost part of their weapon into the pond and the water rippled in increasing circles away from the impact point. We all leaned forward and craned our necks to see who had done it, and the big Ukrainian stood up unemotionally.

"OOhh!" We called again when we realised who it was.

That bloke walked to the end of the bridge and sat down again to remove his boots and socks, calmly placing them together on the ground. He then rolled up his trouser legs and jumped down to the embankment, picking up a big stick by the pond, before wading in slowly, prodding the ground ahead of him as he edged forwards. The crocodiles lay still, watching him from only a few metres away, they were probably as stunned as we were as we looked on in disbelief. When he got to the point where he thought the parts had landed, he prodded around with the pole, then held onto it with one hand for balance, and bent down into a crouch, never taking his eyes off the crocs. Using his other hand, he fished around under the water for a few seconds before standing up triumphantly with the rods and spring firmly in his grasp. We all cheered as he withdrew backwards from the pond and climbed back onto the bridge. He really was hard as nails!

BUGS DON'T BUG ME

My first overseas exercise in the Army was a six-week trip to Kenya in February 1994 with 3 Para. One of the phases was a week-long jungle training package in a training area known as Kathendini, located in the foothills of Mount Kenya. Before leaving the UK, one of the older soldiers who'd been there before advised me to buy a hammock so I wouldn't have to sleep on the jungle floor with all its bugs and critters. I bought a hammock from one of the military equipment shops in Aldershot for an extortionate price and looked forward to sleeping in it for the first time. When we arrived at Kathendini a few weeks into our trip a soldier from the Royal Artillery was attached to my Platoon. His unit was also on exercise and had arranged for some of their blokes to do some training with us for experience. As the new bloke, I was partnered up with him, because nobody else wanted to talk to him, and it was assumed he'd be a pain in the ass. It quickly transpired that he indeed was, when we were told to sort ourselves out and prepare our individual shelters. Taking my hammock from my rucksack I began tying it between two trees a few feet off the ground, as did everyone else after selecting their own space. My new buddy did not have a hammock and told me so.

"You'll have to sleep on the floor then mate." I said.

"I haven't got a poncho either!" he informed me.

A "Poncho" is a waterproof shelter sheet, like a small tarpaulin, that every soldier is issued. When sleeping on the ground they are big enough for 2 men to share, but when using a hammock, they are the right size for a single man.

"Then you better hope it doesn't fucking rain!" I replied unsympathetically.

My Section Commander, Todd had overheard our conversation and interjected. "If he hasn't got a poncho, he'll have to share yours!" He shouted.

I looked at him, frustrated. "For fucks sake! How can you not have a poncho? Are you taking the piss?" I snapped angrily.

I was determined to use my new bit of kit and continued to construct my shelter. "You can sleep underneath me." I suggested.

As soon as he started laying out his equipment beneath my hammock, I could see it wasn't going to work and to the amusement of the others, begrudgingly began to dismantle it and start again, this time using the poncho in a conventional way to fit us both under, lying on the floor. I never did get to use that hammock, but in hindsight it was a piece of crap anyway. I actually gave it to another bloke, who had naively bought the same one, and he used mine to repair his when it broke on the first night, sending him crashing to the floor.

That first night on the jungle floor taught me a couple of things, firstly, invest in a good hammock, and secondly, it's true, if you leave bugs alone, they'll leave you alone.

I was woken up twice that night, the first time by the sound of someone falling from their broken hammock and then by the feeling of something landing on my face. Instinctively I quickly brushed it off with my hand as I shot up into a sitting position. Around my neck I wore a small green torch called a Maglite Solitaire, that had a tiny yellow lightbulb, LED's and headtorches weren't really used back then. Wondering what creature had invaded my space, I held the torch between both thumbs and forefingers and twisted it to turn it on. Forests are pitch black at night so the light it cast was surprisingly good as I focused the beam onto the ground. Propped up on one hand I turned to scan the ground behind me when I saw a huge bug like a cricket or stick insect resting on my hand. Surprised again, I swiped at it and knocked it off my hand with the Maglite, then shone the torch to see where it had landed. At that point I realised it was pointless worrying about that bug because there were bugs everywhere and the light enabled me to see them as they scurried, jumped, and crawled away from the beam. I'd never seen a Wolf Spider until then and learned that their eyes lit up like reflectors when light shone directly at them. I also saw my first ever millipede which was crawling along the floor close to where my head had been resting. For a few seconds I was a bit freaked out, but quickly realised it was well beyond my control, if I were going to worry about the creatures, I'd never get any sleep.

"Fuck it!" I thought, and when the millipede had passed, I got my head back down. I never gave a shit about creepy crawlies again after that, and I've spent many nights on the jungle and desert floors since in lots of places. I'm still shit scared of elephants though!

Topless in Kathendini. My shelter is behind me, propped up by a stick

CAT NAP

The Jamaica Inn is an 18th century coaching inn located high on Bodmin Moor, Cornwall, and is famous for a couple of reasons. Firstly it was the inspiration for Daphne du Maurier's famous novel "The Jamaica Inn," and secondly, it is said to be one of the most haunted pubs in Great Britain. When I worked at the U. K's military survival school, we'd often spend nights there while we ran courses on the moor. The first time I ever stayed there, the lady at reception placed about five keys on the counter for the rooms that were booked for us. Within a flash there was only one key left as the others grabbed them quickly, and I was left with room number 2.

"Whoa, number two. Good luck mate!" said one of the others.

"What do you mean, good luck?" I replied.

The others educated me on the inn and it's ghostly reputation. The rooms were split between the old building and a new annex, with numbers 1-4 being in the old side, and the remainder in the annex.

"That's one of the worst one's!" I was told. "That and number 4!" One of the blokes even told me how he'd been woken up in room number 2 by a ghost that walked right through his bed while he was in it.

I was actually pretty chuffed to be on the old side, because I was open to the idea of ghosts and thought if they were real, I'd get to see one. I never saw one that night but did have a strange encounter a couple of years later.

I was sleeping in a twin room on the ground floor of the annex, when I was woken up by a light pressure pushing down on my chest and the feeling of someone's breath on my lips. When I opened my eyes, I was nose-to-nose with a cat that was stood on my chest, staring right at me. It was a hot summer night, so I was only sleeping under a sheet, and I ran the back of my hand under the sheet towards the cat and flicked it off.

"Fuck off cat!" I said quietly, not wanting to disturb my mate Smudge who was in the next bed. The cat stood still in the space between the beds for a few seconds, before lowering into a crouch then jumping up onto Smudge's mattress. It was about 3 o'clock in the morning and we were getting up in an hour, so I thought it was best to get rid of it before it woke him up. Wearing just a pair of boxer shorts, I stood up and walked over to the cat, which by now had crawled halfway up Smudge's bed, and grabbed hold of it with both hands, but as I lifted it, the cat dug it's claws into the sheet and pulled it away from Smudge. Startled awake, he grabbed the top of the sheet and pulled it back up to his shoulders, looking at me worriedly as I stood over him half-naked with a ball of fur in my hands.

"What are you doing!?" he asked, bleary eyed and confused. He looked like a frightened kid who thought there was a monster in his room.

"It's alright mate." I chuckled. "There's a cat in the room, but I'm getting rid of it."

I carried the cat to the open window and dropped it onto the footpath outside.

"Psssstt!!" I hissed at it to shoe it away, before getting back in my bed and going to sleep.

The following day I mentioned the encounter to one of the ladies in Reception, who immediately ceased organising her files and looked at me intently.

"Was it a black cat?" she asked inquisitively.

It was dark in the room, but I was quite confident. "Yes, I think so." I replied.

The other lady, who'd had her back to me up until this point turned around to look at her workmate and they exchanged a knowing look and slight nod of the head.

"What's that all about?" I said, realising that I was obviously missing something.

The second lady turned around again and faced me.

"It wasn't a cat!" she stated mysteriously.

"Erm, yes it was." I replied.

The first woman shook her head knowingly. "No, it wasn't." she agreed with her friend.

"Okay, what was it then?" I conceded.

The second lady answered. "It's a ghost!" she said sincerely. "It walks around the rooms at night looking for it's master, an old lady who lived here over a hundred years ago."

"Well it felt like a cat when I threw it out the window!" I said dismissively, before walking off.

I used to be open minded about ghosts and even hoped they were real, but after spending so much time there without a sighting I'm a non-believer now. A couple of good friends, who aren't the type to lie, did have experiences that really freaked them out though.

-CHAPTER FIVE-

EVERY DAY'S A
SCHOOL DAY

A FEW DO'S AND DON'TS

In the first few days of recruit training my platoon of about forty young blokes was marched around the different parts of camp to familiarise us with key locations and introduce us to lots of key personalities. One of the places was the Navy, Army and Airforce Institution shop (the NAAFI) which was basically a newsagent that also sold a few cheap and nasty bits of military kit like camouflage cream and waterproof notebooks. The amount of cleaning we did on a daily basis meant the vast majority of our purchases were on bleach, cream cleanser, scouring pads and cloths. Just about everyone also bought an ironing board and an iron too. The NAAFI sold snacks and drinks and we'd go down there to grab a few bits sometimes, to take a few minutes from all the chores we had. It wasn't that simple though, because there were a few unwritten rules and protocols that our instructors made us aware of. One thing we learned was there are certain items in that shop deemed totally unacceptable for us to buy, and if we did, and got caught, we'd be punished. These items were classed as "Hat kit" meaning they were used by non-Parachute Regiment soldiers (Hats) who we were taught to despise. Starch was one such item. "Paratroopers press their kit. Hats need starch because they are weak!" we were informed.

Crisps were another. "Hats eat crisps, that's why they are fat!" they said.

Pot Noodles were particularly hated and treated like some kind of Kryptonite! "Hats eat Pot Noodles, because they are too fucking lazy to cook themselves a proper scoff!" was the party line.

The other problem with going to the NAAFI was a conflict of interest with another shop. One of our Corporals decided to get in on the snacks and drinks business and opened his own "Tuck Shop" which he ran from the staff room when he was on duty in the evenings. He'd shout out really loud "Tuck shops' open!" and would sell cheap brand cola, lemonade, and chocolate bars for higher prices than the decent ones in the NAAFI. One night I sneaked past the staff room and went to the NAAFI to get a newspaper and a packet of biscuits but got caught on the way back.

"Who's that?" he shouted as I crept past.

"Private Brown Corporal!" I said, halting to attention in the corridor.

He came to the door and looked at me with a disappointed expression. Pointing at my NAAFI carrier bag he asked. "What the fuck is that Brown?"

"Just a couple of bits from the NAAFI Corporal." I answered woefully.

"Is my tuck shop not good enough for you Brown?" he asked menacingly.

"I wanted a newspaper Corporal, and you don't sell newspapers, so I went there." I explained.

"Are you saying you don't like what I've got in my shop? Is it not good enough for you Brown?" he responded.

"No Corporal." I said. Whatever I said was going to be wrong.

"I've got some ice-cold cans of coke in here. Are you thirsty? Do you want one or is my coke not good enough either?" he offered. I wasn't thirsty at all. "Yes, please Corporal." I said. "I'll have one."

He disappeared and came back a few seconds later with a room temperature can of Panda Cola (RRP £0.30p) and handed it to me. "That's one pound." He said without a hint of jest.

I paid him and left. I didn't even drink coke, so I gave it away to someone else.

One of the people we were obligated to meet was someone from the Women's Royal Voluntary Service (WRVS) whose office was adjacent to the NAAFI. Before we were marched in and sat down our Corporal told us to be quiet, and not ask any questions. A nice old lady gave us a brief on the history of the service and explained that if we ever felt the need to talk to someone in confidence, they were there for us. She said we might experience homesickness, worry about our families coping without us, and self-doubt during training but these were all perfectly normal feelings, and we were welcome to see her for a cup of tea, a biscuit, and a chat at any time. She also mentioned that the WRVS would help anyone who thought they were being bullied or unfairly treated. When she finished, she asked. "Does anybody have any questions for me?"

No one dared ask anything and we just sat there in silence until the Corporal thanked her for her time and she said her goodbyes then left.

Checking she had gone the Corporal stood out in front of us where she'd been standing and warned us. "Listen in you lot! She is an interfering old bitch, and if any of you fuckers ever speak to her, I will personally knock your fucking teeth out! Do you understand me?"

"Yes Corporal!" We shouted in unison, like a bunch of lunatics.

CRASH COURSE IN SKIING

Learning to ski with 3 Para was definitely a crash course. We played a game of British Bulldog with skis but no poles as our first lesson, then progressed over a few more lessons to the point where we could stop on a slight decline. Within a handful of lessons, we found ourselves heading out to a new training area in our over-snow vehicles called BV 206's. Sat in the back, we looked at each other nervously as we climbed steeply up a hillside for a very long time, eventually flattening out and coming to a halt. When the rear door opened, an instructor ushered us out and we clambered through the doorway before retrieving our skis from the roof and strapping our feet to the bindings. There were probably forty students on that hill and most of us couldn't ski for toffee, we were terrible! One of the instructors briefed us on the exercise ahead as we lined up apprehensively on top of the mountain. Up to that point we had practiced on the flat, and a very small hill / mound. He began by pointing downhill and indicating the location of some buildings at the bottom, about two kilometres away.

"You've got an hour and a half to get to those buildings. See you down there." He instructed then turned and skied skilfully away, closely followed by every other instructor there. There was a long pause as we watched them go and we looked around at each other in disbelief. This hill was massive, and steep, and we were the biggest collection of rubbish skiers ever assembled. After a few seconds it was clear that this was not a joke. The instructors had left, and the vehicles had also turned around and departed.

"Fuck it!" Someone shouted and started to ski, propelling himself forward with both poles and adopting a couching position.

Accelerating rapidly, he managed about 25 metres before losing control and face-planting into the deep snow. This acted like a starting pistol for everyone else and within a couple of seconds we were all following his example, hurtling down the hill like a bunch of maniacs, crashing into rocks, snowdrifts, and each other. I remember watching one bloke shooting past me on my right while I was dusting off the snow from my latest wipe-out. He was attempting to stop, but the snow-plough technique he'd practiced on the mound wasn't proving effective on the mountain at higher speed. Arms flailing, he somehow managed to stay upright as he continued to pick up speed. Ahead of him was a vertical drop of about six foot. "Fucking hell, I can't stop!" He shouted and along with several others I watched with bated breath as he flew over the edge in the most un-elegant display of ski jumping ever performed by a human being. Fortunately, he landed on a nice patch of soft, deep snow and quickly got up, re-fitted his skis which had come off on landing and started again. Eventually we all made it to the bottom and amazingly no one was injured. Maybe those instructors did know what they were doing after all.

During our three months in Norway, we were given the opportunity to try downhill skiing at a civilian ski slope a couple of times. The slope was in a town called Voss and usually there was a British Army adventure training centre there, but our headquarters, in their infinite wisdom decided it wasn't required during our trip. We weren't there to have fun! The first time I went there it was absolute chaos and the blokes were smashing into civilians, tumbling down the slopes and helplessly hanging upside down in trees that lined the routes. Most of us were still unstable on our issue, cross-country NATO planks let alone the much faster downhill skis we'd hired. The closure of the adventure training centre also meant we had no proper clothing, and I wasn't the only one wearing jeans and a fleece jacket, that quickly became covered in snow after numerous falls. The snow stuck to these types of materials and I remember how it would freeze into a crust while sitting on the ski lift and needed to be cracked and broken when dismounting at the top. Whilst sat there one time, ascending the hill, I noticed a single ski falling from the chairlift in front. The bloke who'd lost it was panicking, leaning over to the side to see it sticking out of the snow. Me and my mate were laughing, that was going to be a difficult recovery, especially on one ski! Suddenly a second ski fell from the chair, landing a bit further up the slope than the first, it had been kicked off deliberately. We could hear the two men in front shouting at each other before the one with no skis unbuckled himself and leapt from his seat. We were about fifty feet above the ground, and he dropped like a stone, arms and legs flailing, luckily landing in deep snow, and as we continued our ascent, we passed over the top of him as he waded through the snow towards his skis. It turned out he was a new bloke and was he worried that he'd get in trouble if he lost a ski.

The second time I visited those slopes I dressed much more appropriately in a pair of Ron Hill running tights and a sweatshirt. Over the top I wore the flimsy, white jacket, and trousers we were issued for camouflage, so the snow didn't stick to me when I fell. I must have looked a right plonker, but I didn't care.

Looking a bit unsteady on my army issue "Planks"

INTERNATIONAL RUGBY

I have only played a competitive game of rugby once in my whole life, but at least I can say it was an international! We were on a training exercise in Jordan and had visited the British embassy to have a drink and socialise, when our boss, Liam agreed to play a "friendly" game against the local rugby team. They called themselves Jordan Rugby Club although several of their players were British ex-pats that also frequented the embassy. On hearing about the match, it became clear that I wasn't the only one with zero knowledge or experience of rugby. Most of us didn't even know the rules.

"Why don't we have a game of football instead?" we asked. "At least everyone knows how to play football!"

There were a few of the blokes that played rugby, some were even on the local team in Stowmarket, and with their support the boss stuck to his agreement.

"We're playing rugby!" he confirmed. That was that.

The next morning, instead of going for a run, we had rugby training. Supervised by one of the enthusiasts called "Tricky," we gathered on the tennis court for our induction and over an hour we learned what position we would play in, how to do a line-out and that the ball had to be passed backwards, not forwards. We were ready!

The day of the match we drove through the capital city Amman, following directions to the sports ground. We'd been there a while so were no longer shocked by the number of stray dogs that roamed the streets or lay dead in the gutters and concentrated on the route. Heading away from the centre there was a huge building ahead, and as we drove, we got closer and closer to it.

"I hope we're not going there!" I said, pointing at what appeared to be a grand stadium. My head was filled with visions of us playing in there, watched by thousands of proud Jordanians baying for our blood. This could turn into a national humiliation! The stadium got closer still, and it was obviously our destination. We stopped in a sandy car park adjacent to the building and were greeted by someone from the embassy. We weren't playing in the stadium; we were playing on training pitch next to the car park. It didn't look like a pitch though, it looked like a piece of flat desert with rugby posts at either end. It wasn't ploughed to soften the hard baked surface and it hadn't been cleared of stones and rocks either. At the far end the Jordanian team were warming up, running around in figure of eights, passing the ball side to side. They looked like they knew what they were doing, and they looked very smart in their team kit. We, on the other hand were wearing our running shorts, maroon t-shirts, and trainers, and we looked total amateurs as we did some arm-circles and a couple of lunges as our preparation. Liam was approached by one of the oppositions players.

"You need to get changed into your kit." He advised.

"We don't have one." Replied Liam. "We're playing in this." he said, pointing to his attire.

The man looked concerned, our flimsy running clothes would get torn to shreds, we'd be naked within seconds! "Wait here, I'll see what I can do." He said before re-joining his teammates. Five minutes later a vehicle arrived, and we were given the Jordanians' away-kit, which we donned gratefully.

Rugby is normally played in two halves of 40 minutes each but even our half-hearted warm up made us realise we couldn't last that long without a water break. It was red hot; the sun was beating down from high in the sky and the ground and nearby buildings seemed to be reflecting the heat even more. We asked the referee if we could play 4 twenty-minute quarters instead and he authorised it after consulting with the Jordanians. Looking at their team it was obvious that we were the fitter side, we were all in good shape and had some fast runners as well as a few big strong lads that liked the gym. The other team just looked like a bunch of civvies that would probably die if they attempted our fitness regime. However, due to them understanding the basics of rugby gameplay and tactics, despite their evident lack of aerobic capacity they beat us 27-0 in a game where we did a lot of running around / chasing the ball, and they did a lot of passing.

On the Jordanian team there was one man who stood out from the rest. He was massive! Standing well over six-feet tall, he looked like a stereotypical rugby player with broad shoulders, tree trunk legs, cauliflower ears and a broken nose. At one point in the game, I found myself directly in between him and our goalposts as he charged towards our touchline at an impressive speed. If I could have bluffed my way out of it I would, but he didn't even try to go around me, instead just accelerated straight at me like an angry bull. During our practice I had asked Tricky about this exact scenario.

"What do you do if someone is coming straight at you?" I'd asked him. "Do you go for the ankles, legs or waist?"

"Here." He replied pointing to my mid-section.

"And do I tackle head-on, or from the side as they go past?" I continued.

"Straight-on, with your shoulder! Like this." Tricky explained, demonstrating the position on one of the other blokes. "Hit them hard and fold them in half!" He said matter-of-factly.

His advice was no doubt correct, but probably works better if you commit to it with confidence and aren't on the wrong side of a 4-stone weight disadvantage. That bloke hit me like a freight train, and I was propelled backwards when his thigh slammed into my chest at about 20mph, knocking me clear off my feet, landing on my back. I lay there for a second in a bit of a daze, my head had been snapped backwards and bounced off the floor on landing, I thought I probably had whiplash. Tricky ran past me.

"Come on, get up!" he shouted as he chased after the giant, followed by the remainder of the team. We really should have played a game of football.

After the match we all had some food and drinks while a video of the game played in the background on a big television. I wasn't the only one to get hurt, some of our blokes had bite marks, scratches, and stud imprints on their legs from the Jordanians boots.

Friendly game my arse!

Before the game in the away-kit from the other team

THE LANGUAGE BARRIER

Just like different parts of the UK have their own accents, colloquialisms, and dialects, so do the Armed Forces, and in order to understand who, what, when, why, where, and how you are being told to do something, you need to learn it quickly. In the Navy, "shipmates" eat their "scran" in the "galley", in the Army "the blokes" get "scoff" in the "cookhouse", and in the Royal Air Force those bloody good chaps take luncheon in the jolly old cafeteria. The Navy call their lingo "Jack speak" and it's like an entire language that dates back hundreds of years and is steeped in history and tradition. I was sat at scoff with a Royal Marine once who loved a bit of Jack speak and when I stood up with my empty bowl, he looked at me with a grin and said. "Round the boy?"

My hearing isn't the best, so I thought I might have misheard him. "Say again mate." I replied.

"Round the boy is it?" he repeated.

My poor hearing has given me an ability to work out what people are saying by piecing things together and lip reading but I was stumped. "What do you mean?" I asked.

"Double duff?" he said.

I knew he wasn't trying to wind me up because he was a really nice bloke. I looked at him blankly. "Mate, I have no idea what you are talking about." I admitted.

There was a second of awkward silence as he tried to think of the words, but instead just said it again, pointing at the hotplate and my bowl. "Round the boy, for a double duff!" he chuckled.

The gestures did the trick. "Are you asking me if I'm going up for seconds?" I said.

He nodded and had a little laugh at the "Pongo" (army soldier) with the others at the table. "Yes mate." He replied.

"Fucking Marines!" I joked, shaking my head. "Why didn't you just say that you weirdo?" In Jack speak "Duff" is dessert / pudding and going "Round the buoy" is doing something twice.

I'm as guilty as him though because I've confused plenty of people with army lingo, although our vocabulary is tiny compared to theirs. I went into the NAAFI shop on camp once and couldn't find what I was looking for because they had rearranged the layout of the shelves. Approaching the shop attendant, I asked them. "Excuse me mate, where is the dhobi dust?"

"The what!?" he asked. He was new.

"The dhobi dust." I repeated, not even considering he might not understand me. "I think it's been moved."

"What is dhobi dust?" he queried.

At that point I realised that I didn't know either. I had never bought it as a civilian, my mum did the shopping, and the washing when I lived at home. I must have looked a right moron to him as I racked my brains to think what it's civvy designation was, but I couldn't think. Instead, I just blurted out some brand names. "You know, Daz, Ariel, erm Persil." I explained with my hands out in front of me like I was holding a box of the stuff.

"Do you mean washing powder?" he guessed correctly.

I wasn't really sure. I hadn't heard it called that for years, but it sounded like it might be right. I wasn't sure if washing powder was the stuff you used to wash, but then remembered that was washing-up liquid.

"Yeah, that's it." I replied.

He pointed to the back of the shop. "It's down there on the right." He said.

Another time I was at a Mongolian wok restaurant in Oxford on a Stag Night when I noticed everyone was eating with chopsticks. I spent about four years eating with just a spoon in 3 Para and my dexterity with that is second-to-none, but I've never seen the point in learning to eat with chopsticks. Looking around I couldn't see a spoon, so I got the attention of a waiter who came over.

"Excuse me mate, have you got any diggers please?" I requested.

"Any what sir?" he said,

"Diggers." I repeated.

The blank look on his face made me realise he didn't know what I was on about, but I couldn't remember the word, so I just mimed instead, and motioned like I was prodding my food with a knife and fork as I said, "Dig-gers."

The mime clearly worked. "Cutlery?" he suggested.

"Correct answer!" I replied.

He bought over a load of diggers and most of the others abandoned their chopsticks to join me in eating like an ignorant party pooper too, except they used knives and forks and I just used the spoon, like a right tramp.

One bloke who always took it a stage too far was Dave, (Shitto Man) and he had a special set of diggers to beat them all. Often the blokes will do an "all-in" scoff in the field, where everyone adds their rations to a big pot, usually to make a curry or a chilli, which they all share from. This is when the "Racing Spoons" come out, and everyone eyes up the competition to see what they're packing. You'd get a wide variety including wooden spoons, Chinese bowl spoons, sporks, and some good size dessert spoons. If you were stupid enough to bring a small spoon to the party, you'd get less scoff, and if you were a culinary amateur like me that couldn't handle hot sauces or curry powders, or like me, ate slowly, you would go hungry. Dave's diggers even had names and it was hilarious when you saw him deploy them at scoff time. The "Hoof" was his spoon, and it was a full-size metal serving spoon that you'd only expect to see at a hotplate. The "Claw" was his fork, which was a full-size meat carving fork that resembled a small trident.

TERMINOLOGY

Civilian	Paratrooper	Context
Civilian	Civvy	Civvies will never understand you
New soldier	Joe / Crow / Joseph / Crowseph / Zepster	Crows do all the crappy jobs
Lance Corporal	Lance-Jack	One day you crows might be Lance-Jacks
Corporal	Full-Screw	One day you Lance-Jacks might be Full Screws
Sergeant	Sarn't (**Not** "Sarge or Sargey")	Yes Sarn't, no Sarn't, three bags full Sarn't
Colour Sergeant	Colour-Man	Go and see the Colour-Man to collect some Norwegians
Company Sergeant Major	CSM	Report to the CSM's office. You are in the shit!
Regimental Sergeant Major	RSM / The Badge	Report to the RSM. You are severely in the shit!
Junior officer (Second Lieutenant)	One pip wonder	What do they know? The one pip wonder has only been in the army 5 minutes
Junior officer (Lieutenant)	Two pip wonder	What do they know? The two-pip wonder has only been in the army 10 minutes
Soldier who is nice to recruits	Foj (Friend of Joe)	Were you showing the crows how to

		iron their smocks? You Foj!
Non-Parachute Regiment soldier	Craphat / Hat / Harry boy / Screamer / Haraldo / Non-ferocious	Do not talk to the non-ferocious, screaming Haraldo Craphats
Territorial Army	T.A	He's in the T.A, he plays soldiers at the weekends
T.A soldier	S.T.A.B	Be quiet you STAB
Idiot / moron	Mong	That Mong doesn't know one end of his weapon from the other
A stickler for the rules	Straight bloke / Laser beam	He wears his beret like a right straight bloke / Laser
Camp / effeminate man	Strrraaiight bloke!	We found a Justin Bieber calendar and a strap-on dildo in his locker, strrraaiight bloke!
Someone who reads military publications	Pamphlet head	That platoon is full of straight bloke, pamphlet heads
Married soldier	Pad	He's not coming out tonight because he's a stinking pad
Cigarette	Bine	If you want a bine, go outside
Smoker	Biner	You stinking biners can smoke over there
Canteen / Dining area / Restaurant	Cookhouse	The Cookhouse opens at 0600hrs for scoff
Food / Meal	Scoff	Get some scoff down your neck
Tea / coffee	Brew	Get yourself a brew

		or some screech
Squash / Cordial	Screech	Get yourself some screech or a brew
Large flask for scoff, screech, or brews	Norwegian	I can taste yesterday's scoff in the brew from the Norwegian
Cutlery	Diggers	There's no diggers in the cookhouse so take your own
Knife, fork, spoon	KFS	Don't forget your KFS
Washing up	Doing dixies / Pan bashing	I need 3 crows from the Company to do the Dixies
Fuel pump	POL	Go to the POL and fill up some jerry cans with diesel
Wash / Dirty washing	Dhobi	Get your dirty kit in the dhobi
Missing / Lost / Deficient	Diffy	He was talking when he should have been listening, and now he's diffy a few teeth
Clean / polish to a high standard	Bull	Bull your boots till you can see your reflection in them
Ceremonial / traditional nonsense	Bullshit	Paint the scorched grass green because there's a Royal visit
Physical fitness	PT	P.T is at 0800hrs
Speed march / load carry	Tab	There's no transport so we're tabbing there
Easy / spare	Buckshee	That was a buckshee run / Has anyone got any buckshee dhobi dust?
Give up / person who	Jack	Don't jack on your

gives up		fitness / He jacked on the 10 miler
Safety vehicle	Jack wagon	Catch up or you'll be going on the Jack wagon
Hard fitness session	Beasting	That run was a beasting
Cool / different / impressive	Ally	The way paratroopers wear their kit is ally
The art of being ally	Allyness	Paratrooper allyness is level 10, Marines level 2
Rucksack	Bergan	Bergans on! Let's go!
Desert boots	DB's	Order of dress; Para Reg t-shirt, jeans and DB's
Jacket	Smock	Big baggy smocks are ally
Civilian clothes	Civvies	Bring a set of civvies in case we get a night off
Split up	Bomb burst	We all bomb burst when the police turned up
Do me a favour / Take it easy	Screw the nut	"Screw the nut, tell the police I was with you last night." / "This run won't be too fast; I'm going to screw the nut."
When a parachute collapses because the parachute below it steals the air required to inflate	Air steal	His canopy collapsed because he got caught in an air steal

THINKING YOU'RE THE BEST ISN'T THE SAME AS KNOWING YOU ARE

The pride of being a paratrooper was always very special to me, and still is. The hardships we endure to earn that honour are beyond a lot of people's comprehension, even other soldiers, although they might not know it. As a young paratrooper I was fully indoctrinated like many other impressionable youths who have gone through Depot Para, then spent years in a Battalion reinforcing their opinions. I remember in the early days of our courtship I was talking to my wife, probably about how I hated people, and fed up, she said. "Who do you like Steve? You hate civvies, you hate soldiers who aren't in your Regiment, you hate officers. Is there anyone you do like?"

I thought about it for a second before answering. "You're alright." I replied dryly.

Once, on a promotion course, I was sat next to a soldier from the Fusiliers, and it wasn't long before I was educating him on why the Parachute Regiment was the best. In his defence he did stick up for his unit, but only through a sense of duty.

"What do you think is the best Regiment in the British Army?" I asked.

"The Fusiliers." He stated.

"Seriously? You honestly think you are better than the Parachute Regiment?" I challenged.

He answered loyally. "Well I'm in the Fusiliers, so I'm going to say the Fusiliers aren't I!"

I was on him like a rash. "Forget about that, I'm not asking who you think you *should* say, I'm asking who you really think is the best. Who you would want standing alongside you in a fight to the death." I said.

I suppose that would be the Paras." He admitted.

That is the difference between Para Reg soldiers and the majority of others, because paratroopers have a true and total belief in themselves as a fighting force. They will not even consider another unit as their equal and that is why they chose to join that Regiment in the first place, because it is the best, because it is the hardest challenge. People join other units for many other reasons such as, it's their local Regiment, or it provides them with a trade, and often their reason for not attempting Para Reg is that it is too hard. In my experience there is only one other unit that holds a similar self-belief and esprit de corps; The Royal Marines. But.......... they're wrong.

On that same course I was sat at the back of a 4-ton troop carrying vehicle as we drove through a Welsh town. Following behind us was a car with two attractive women in it who were acting a bit giggly. When we turned into a junction they gave a nice smile and wave as they continued along the road we'd left. The soldier sat next to me was very pleased with himself.

"See that? They were waving at me!" He exclaimed. "They want a piece!"

To me it looked like they'd just been looking in our general direction, which was hard to avoid because we were right in front of them, but I wasn't about to admit that.

"What do you think they saw when they looked in the back of this wagon?" I asked him.

He paused for thought.

"They saw a paratrooper!" I boasted, before he could even answer, pointing to my head dress. "They looked at us, and all they saw was my beret and my cap badge."

"No mate, I'm pretty sure they were looking at me." He said.

I explained my conclusion. "I can go anywhere in the world, and people will look at me and know straight away that I'm a para-trooper, but even I don't know what your cap badge is!" He was from the Duke of Wellington's Regiment who's history dated back to 1702A.D, two hundred and forty years before the Paras, but not as famous.

"Do you really think that's true?" he asked me.

"Fuckin right it is!" I answered cockily.

"Shit! I need to get myself one of those berets." He sighed.

BEST ADVICE EVER

In 1983, when I was nine years old I met my friend Karl and we've been good friends ever since, even though we hardly saw each other once I joined the Army. We both loved the martial arts and used to spar together from an early age, punching lumps out of each other in his garage or my bedroom. He was far more talented than me though and was a champion in kick boxing and nunchaku. Karl's dad Brian Downton used to watch sometimes, and he'd laugh at us when we re-entered the house with black eyes and bloody noses. A tough Yorkshireman from Castleford, Brian had spent time down the mines and been a powerlifting champion, and I used to see him out running on cold winter nights, wearing his black woolly hat. I always looked up to him and he taught me how to lift weights, showed me running routes, and even loaned me his training equipment so I could train at home, he was my first mentor and a proper old-school hard nut. One day after I'd been in the army for a short while I paid Brian a visit, and he asked me if I'd kept up my training. I'd been busy on exercises and my cardio was very good, but I had neglected my resistance training.

"I haven't done any weights for a while." I confessed.

He was surprised. "Eh? Why not?"

"I haven't been able to get to a gym that much."

His face said it all as he shook his head slightly. I knew I'd fucked up and felt ashamed, I was bullshitting myself and him.

"There's always a floor Steve!" he said. "There's always a bloody floor!"

He was right, there is always a floor, so there is never an excuse.

"Sorry Brian." I said respectfully. "There's no excuse."

"You can always do your push ups and sit ups son. Don't ever stop training." He told me.

That was probably the best advice I have ever been given by anyone, not only because it incentivises me to train, but also stops me from making excuses not to. If you really want to train, there is no reason not to. There's always an excuse, but there's also always a floor. I have used that advice on other people loads of times and always accredit it to Brian, you can't argue with it. He gave me another piece of advice once when his wife Brenda came in and asked him to do something for her that he obviously didn't relish.

"Aye alright love." He said reluctantly. "I'll be there in a minute." As Brenda left the room he looked at me and said "Just keep nodding son. Keep bloody nodding." He was right again, and they are still happily married to this day. Awesome couple.

-PSYCHOTHERAPY-

THE POT CALLS THE KETTLE BLACK

My father called me a coward once. As a soldier it doesn't get much worse than that! We'd had an explosive argument the previous time we met, and afterwards I'd sent him an email to explain my side of the story. He knew I was struggling with my mental health and I'd been open and honest, telling him things that were bothering me and asking some questions. The reason I sent the email was that discussion had failed, we were unable to communicate because he was so defensively aggressive and unwilling to talk. No doubt he would blame me too, but I'd stand by my assessment of the situation.

"Your email!" he said pointing in my face angrily, "I call it your vilemail! How dare you send me that vilemail like a coward! That's what you are, a coward, hiding behind your vilemail!"

I'd lost my temper the last time we argued and had vowed not to this time.

"I'm a coward, am I?" I responded, nodding my head. "I'm a coward?" I repeated, pointing to my own chest. "You let your own children live in fear of another man and did nothing about it! You let another man force your children to flee their own house in terror and did fuck all to help them!" I said. "You are the coward, not me!" I pointed to my car where my own kids were sitting and asked him. "Do you think I would ever let someone frighten my children like that? Do you think I would ever let anyone do that to them?"

Surprisingly, he answered me honestly. "No, I don't." He admitted.

"Fucking right I wouldn't! I'd fucking kill them and bury them on the Moor! You are the coward!" I snarled, angered by the mere thought of it.

After that visit, like the one before it, I spent the entire 230-mile drive home to Cornwall feeling angry, sad, and confused. My wife could see how negatively he was affecting me, but thankfully never stoked the fire, she didn't defend him, but she didn't excuse him either, she just tried to assure me that I'd done nothing wrong. I visited him once more after that, and that also ended badly. He suggested we take our dogs for a walk and I agreed, taking my kids along too. It was all going okay until I asked him what he thought happened to my dog when I was a kid and he lost the plot again, admitting that he thought Terry had killed her, but making it clear I wasn't allowed to ask questions. I'd only continued going there so he could see his grandchildren, but I stopped after that when I realised, he just made me feel bad. I don't even talk to him on the phone now, we're done.

-CHAPTER SIX-

NO SHIT I COULD HAVE DIED

AVALANCHES ARE TERRIFYING

In 1997 I was in Norway with 3 PARA when I had one of the most frightening experiences of my life. Five of us had been tasked to carry out a communications recce in one of the training areas to test the capabilities of our radio equipment. Our primary means of communication was notoriously unreliable at night in the Arctic, so we set up camp to test it over 24hrs. Once finished we packed up our equipment into our backpacks and a sled that we dragged behind us. The sled or "Pulk" as it was called was filled with a tent, several radios and batteries and several other bits of survival equipment. All of us could ski to a basic level but only one bloke was good enough to attach himself to the pulk and control it, as it was very heavy and difficult to manoeuvre. He was a military ski instructor which basically meant he was less likely to wipe out than the rest of us. On top of the mountain the weather had closed-in to almost a whiteout, so we stayed close together as we skied off and started our descent under the command of our Sergeant Major. Visibility improved as we gradually lost altitude and after a while, we could see the bottom of the valley and some buildings where we were expecting to be picked up by vehicles later. The route down to the rendezvous point was a treeless slope, much steeper than the previous terrain, dropping away at an angle of about 60 degrees for at least a kilometre. The Sergeant Major realised that we were nowhere near competent enough to negotiate the hill while carrying all our equipment and instructed us to traverse our way down in a long zig-zag fashion. I was fourth in line with the Sergeant Major leading, the pulk puller following him and another soldier holding on to the pulk's brake rope behind him. As we moved along the slope with the low ground on our right side, I noticed a few small snowballs rolling down the hill towards me, leaving a small trail in the snow behind them as they bounced lightly across the gradient. From the training we'd been given I recognised them as "sun-balls."

In the army soldiers are issued with specific aide memoires when deployed to extreme environments such as the desert, jungle or arctic and in the arctic version there is a chapter on avalanches. In that book I'm pretty sure it said that avalanches usually occur on slopes with a gradient between 30-60 degrees, and even more likely if there were no trees to anchor the snow. One of the warnings of an avalanche described was sun-balling where small amounts of snow were breaking away and rolling downhill. I shouted to the bloke in front of me to let him know about the sun-balling and he acknowledged it. Suddenly there was a big booming sound and the ground beneath my skis seemed to drop several inches immediately followed by a loud cracking noise on my left, like the sound of ice splitting on a frozen lake. I instinctively turned towards the sound and could clearly see a crack in the snow above me that looked about a foot wide. Everyone froze, we all thought the entire hillside was going to go, taking us with it. After a few seconds we all started to quickly go through the drills we had practiced, albeit with a sense of urgency, and I loosened my ski bindings and took my rucksack strap from one shoulder. This was also in the aide memoire and was to minimise the injuries the skis and rucksack would cause if caught in the avalanche. Some other advice was to attempt to stay on top of the tonnes of cascading snow by performing a "double-backstroke" swimming action with your arms.

The bloke pulling the pulk was most at risk and he quickly unbuckled himself from inside the metal frame that attached him to the heavy sled. The Sergeant Major instructed the two blokes with the pulk to jettison it. It was by far the heaviest piece of kit and its mass cutting through the snow was probably the most likely thing to trigger a slab avalanche. As best they could the two soldiers nervously manhandled the pulk until it was pointing straight down the mountain, towards the cabins in the valley bottom. Knowing that the contents were worth thousands of pounds they looked toward the Sergeant Major one last time. "Do it." He said.

We all watched apprehensively as that pulk hurtled down the hill, accelerating like a drag car in a straight line down the mountainside. Somehow that pulk stayed upright all the way down, performing a few jumps as it went then slowing down as the gradient flattened and finally stopping when it crashed into a big rock. Amazingly, the radios and other equipment survived intact, but the front of the pulk was smashed. I was scared, but still well impressed with that performance. I really thought the whole hillside was going to detach at any second and my double-backstroke was only slightly better than my butterfly stroke, I had no chance. Under the leadership of the Sergeant Major we quietly and steadily made our way down the mountainside in a slow zig zag, eventually reaching the bottom and retrieving the pulk. While we were waiting for our pickup two men appeared on skis wearing bright red and yellow ski suits. They came over to where we were sitting and asked if everything was ok. It turned out they were mountain rescue volunteers, and they were out to make sure people weren't out on the hills skiing because there was a high avalanche risk.

No shit?!

RPG? WHAT RPG?

Land Rovers are a great bit of kit and can drive through just about anything, but when they are overloaded with water, fuel, weapons, and ammunition their performance understandably deteriorates. In Afghanistan vehicle chassis were regularly getting bent and cracked under the strain being placed on them during patrols across the unforgiving terrain. During one patrol we found ourselves in an area where the ground was so soft the wagons were constantly sinking up to the axles which massively hampered our progress and also made us vulnerable to attack as we got the shovels and recovery kits out to extract them, which was hard work in the heat. While digging out one of the vehicles we received a message that re-tasked us to a new mission in support of an attack to the south. Three hundred men from the Afghan Army and Police were preparing to clear the Taliban from a town with the help of a small British Operational Mentoring and Liaison Team (OMLT) and we were tasked to observe and report any Taliban movement on or across the bridge in the town. Receiving the order, I was initially sceptical that we'd be able to get there on time, because of the distance and the trouble we were having negotiating the terrain, but we managed to get through the soft ground and found a route that afforded us better manoeuvrability. No sooner had we regained some momentum though, than one of the vehicles had a mechanical problem that forced us to stop.

Pathfinder patrols invariably have qualified vehicle mechanics within the team, and it didn't take long for ours to establish we needed a clutch replacement, a big job that not only required a new clutch but lifting equipment as well. Driving slowly and carefully we moved to a hard, flat area where we secured a helicopter landing site (HLS) and waited for an R.A.F Chinook to deliver the parts we needed, plus two mechanics from the Royal Electrical and Mechanical Engineers (REME) to conduct the work. Fair play to those blokes, because they grafted and got the job done, right there in the middle of the desert and within a few hours we were ready to go again. Still in the same positions from when they were dropped off, we called in another Chinook to extract the REME guys and spoke directly to the crew as they approached, bracing ourselves for the inevitable sandblasting from the powerful rotor blade downwash. The dust kicked up and swirled around as the helicopter hovered overhead momentarily before lowering slowly towards the marker, we had placed on the ground for them. Unexpectedly the Chinook rose quickly and flew away into the distance.

Me and Danny looked at each other. "They didn't land, did they?" I asked him.

"I don't think so mate." he said.

Using my radio, I called Scotty for an update, he had been talking to the crew.

"They said they can't land here and they're RTB!" (returning to base) he told me.

"Why can't they land?" I queried. "What did they say exactly?"

Scotty explained how the pilot had declared the landing site was unsuitable and there was too much sand, before abandoning the attempt and the two mechanics. It was difficult for us to understand because the previous crew had already landed there with no problems, and sand seemed to be a fairly obvious and unavoidable nuisance in the desert. After gathering the relevant information, I informed HQ, who were as perturbed as us and told me to wait while they organised another lift. After a short while HQ got back to me to say another lift was unavailable until the following morning, which was too late, so I should carry on as tasked to the bridge. After talking to the REME guys and HQ we made space in the back of two vehicles for them to sit, gave them some ammunition and headed back into the desert, leaving their expensive, but cumbersome equipment behind.

Driving through the night using night vision goggles we were behind schedule but doing our best to get to the target area on time, and when we got within a couple of kilometres of the town, I saw a large gathering of vehicles in the distance. Halting to identify who they were we watched through our various viewing aids, utilising thermal imagers and telescopic night sights as we made calls on the radio to find out if they were friend or foe. We quickly established that it was the Afghan army and ensured that they were aware of our presence to avoid fratricide before continuing on the route we had planned from the map study. As per every map we had, the map of the town didn't quite match what was on the ground, because the buildings had spread out since they were printed, and we started to see small buildings and compound walls earlier than anticipated. By this time, the Sun wasn't far from breaching the horizon and it wasn't long before first light, so I decided to stop briefly and swap the night vision kit from our weapons for daytime ones and stow away our night vision goggles. If we got attacked from the compounds, I didn't want to be faffing around changing kit over. I had just removed the night-scope from my vehicle-mounted machine gun when I got a call from my Light Electronic Warfare Team (LEWT.) There were four of them and they worked round the clock, scanning the airwaves to intercept radio traffic, and using the interpreter to translate anything they captured. The team commander, Dave alerted me. "I've just intercepted a call between two men, and one said; They are coming, we are ready." He was talking quietly, but I could hear the concern in his voice. He continued, correctly anticipating my question. "They could be talking about the bigger group to our south, but I can't confirm. That's all we heard."
We were about to enter an area where we were channelled on either side by long compound walls that flanked us a few hundred metres away so hearing this was a bit unnerving. If the radio

chat were indeed about us, we could be driving into an ambush, but there was no way of telling, and you can't abort a mission just because you think someone might shoot at you. In fact, you spend most of your time on tour anticipating or expecting to be shot at. It was also more likely that the message had been about the large group of Afghan police and army that had also began moving in closer to the town to their form-up-position. It could have been about them, us, someone else we didn't know about, or even a complete bluff.

Cautiously we moved forward slowly across the bumpy ground, my vehicle leading. Half a kilometre later we learned that it probably us they were waiting for when an RPG whooshed towards us from the left and exploded in front of my vehicle, accompanied by bursts of automatic fire with red tracer rounds that cracked overhead. I immediately swung my machine gun mount over to the left and returned fire to where the shots were coming from, aiming at the muzzle flashes of the enemy weapons and my rear gunner Craig did the same. Within a few seconds my next vehicle, whose rear gun was a .50cal Heavy Machine Gun, was also firing, closely followed by the other eight vehicles in the patrol, a total of twenty machine guns. As soon as we had support, my driver Danny began the drill we'd rehearsed a hundred times before to get us out of the killing zone as fast as possible. Ditches and mounds made it impossible to turn around in one movement, so he reversed quickly to begin a three-point-turn. Behind us was a large mound of excavated earth and we went a few feet up it, unbalancing the wagon momentarily. It was on our left side and blind to Danny.
I turned towards him between bursts of fire as he changed gear. "Go steady mate, take your time. We don't want to roll the wagon." I said.
"I'm good mate." He replied. "I just didn't see that one."
"Nice one mate, good skills." I said, as he moved us forward and completed the U-turn.
"You can't teach that!" Danny joked, pleased with his man-

oeuvre.

Even in that moment I remember thinking how casual our conversation was, and I think it was probably quite reassuring for both of us that the other one wasn't flapping. There were rounds flying all around us, but we were talking like he was doing a reverse park in Tesco car park. Events like that are what has convinced me the importance of drills and rehearsals because that contact drill we executed as a ten-vehicle patrol was textbook and enabled us to get everyone out of the danger area quickly and safely and into a rally point where we could reassess the situation. I turned around to talk to Craig in the back, he was also my radio operator and direct link to HQ. "Send a contact report please Craig." I said.

"Done mate." He replied.

"Already! When?" I asked. He had been firing the whole time and when we were moving, he'd have been getting bounced around, holding on tight.

Craig nodded towards the area we'd come from. "I sent it straight away, back there."

He was cool as a cucumber and had sent the report during the firefight.

Happy we were out of range of the enemy gunfire we settled down in a small depression in the ground to check ourselves and equipment for damage when we saw a rocket shooting towards us from the town. Whoever fired it was probably doing it for the first time because we watched it hit the ground a couple of hundred metres short and bounce across the desert floor harmlessly, failing to explode on impact. Soon after that a mortar bomb landed about 200 metres to the north, creating a small black cloud as it, hit then another hit the ground about 200 metres to the south. For a minute I thought they had some mortaring skills as they appeared to be bracketing us. "Prepare to move!" I called out. If the next bomb was closer, we needed to get out of there. The next bomb landed about half a mile away in the middle of nowhere, followed by several more so we just laughed and stayed where we were. They were crap at mortaring! Later on, one of the blokes was talking to me about the firefight.

Fuck me, that RPG was close mate! he said. I remembered it going off to the front right of my vehicle, it was close, but not that close, the killing zone of the blast area is only small. "It wasn't that close!" I said.

"Fuck off! It went right over your bonnet!" he insisted.

"No mate, it landed about 25 metres away to our front right." I replied.

Danny interjected. "Not that one Steve, he means the second one."

"What, there were two?" I said, surprised. "I remember one!"

Danny was laughing. "You were too busy getting rounds down on the GPMG, it went right over the fucking bonnet mate!" He chuckled.

A similar thing happened to a mate of mine in Iraq in 2003 when one of our patrols was involved in a big firefight on a road. An account of the mission is written in a book called "Pathfinder" by Dave Blakely, but I remember when I first saw the blokes after the event and one of them, called Cam was showing me his vehicle and all the bullet holes in it. It was a miracle nobody was hit because there were obviously plenty of near misses. Even the drivers were shooting during that one, with one hand on the steering wheel and the other firing their pistols. When I said how lucky he was to be alive Cam told me that the vehicle in front were even luckier, because an RPG round had flown straight between their front and rear wheels and out the other side!

STOP FLAPPING

They used to say that a parachute malfunction occurs about once in every thousand freefall jumps. In my time at Pathfinders, I did about 450, which is a tiny amount when compared to a recreational skydiver but a fair few in the British military with our lack of resources and prevailing weather conditions. In that 450 I had two "reserve rides," which is when you cut away your main canopy and deploy your reserve parachute. With hindsight and experience I may have been a bit hasty with the first, but the second was a lucky escape. The first time was during my Military Freefall Course in Yuma, Arizona on the GQ360 parachute. I remember pulling the big silver handle and feeling the tug of the parachute as it began to deploy. After completing my compulsory count of "One thousand, two thousand, three thousand check canopy!" I looked up to see a partially deployed canopy that was flapping violently above me. Thinking I'd counted too fast I looked down before looking back up. I'll never know if it was going to open properly but at the time it felt like I had given it plenty of opportunity and decided to pull my reserve. That worked and I quickly had a nice 22-foot round parachute above my head and landed with my feet and knees together, executing a good parachute landing fall. On recovery I was questioned on my reasons for pulling the reserve and the instructors were happy that I did it justifiably. Back then we were deploying at about 3000ft so there wasn't that much time to make a decision. A few years later the standard height for opening increased to 5000ft and I got used to allowing much longer for the parachute to pay out when I experienced "slow openers."

The other time I pulled my reserve was when I had a malfunction known as a "Horseshoe." The GQ360 parachute worked on a kicker-spring system that fired out a small drogue from the pack. That drogue would then catch the air as you fell and drag out the main canopy which would then open. A regular occurrence with that system was that the kicker spring would fire, but not pull out the main, instead it would sit in the "dead air" above your back and flutter about until it caught some air and got pulled away. Sometimes, while it fluttered you could feel it bashing you on the back of the head or hitting your feet and legs. This was a widely accepted possibility and there were drills taught to counter it such as dipping your shoulder on one side to allow the flow of air across your back and whacking the side of the pack with your elbows to encourage the parachute out.

I was in this situation and had done the shoulder rolls and the back-elbows to no avail. I checked my altimeter, by this point I was already at 2000ft, which meant I was about 10 seconds from impact with the ground. I grabbed my cut-away handle and reserve handle and pulled them in quick succession, returning to the freefall position. Nothing happened, I was still in freefall. I tried the shoulder roll and elbows again. Still nothing. I grabbed the cable that ran from the reserve handle in my left hand into the cable housing on my chest and pulled it with both hands as far as it would go and saw the end of the wire. My freefall position had gone out the window now and I was tumbling out of control when suddenly I felt the unmistakeable yank of a canopy opening and looked up to see another 22-foot round parachute above my head. In tow and following us down was a deflated main parachute. I was only a few hundred feet above the ground when I looked down to assess which way I was drifting and realised I was descending towards some power lines between two huge masts. Luckily, the wind was in my favour and I landed about 100m away from them. Back then we'd freefall with our rucksacks attached to the backs of our legs, instead of in front and when I landed, I sat on my pack and flipped over backwards, landing on my ass.

"Dickhead!" I said out loud. In all the excitement I'd forgotten to lower my equipment, I was lucky not to break my legs.

Within a couple of minutes, a vehicle arrived to recover me with two RAF blokes I knew on board. They were our parachute equipment fitters and good lads. One of them told me how they had been counting the canopies as they deployed and noticed one was missing when someone pointed out mine in the distance and already close to the ground.

I had left the parachutes where they fell and sat on my rucksack to take on some water.

The packers looked at the entanglement and explained what had happened. When the main canopy got stuck and I pulled the reserve, the reserve kicker spring had wrapped around the main kicker spring which had prevented it from deploying. Luckily at some point one, or both caught enough air to pull everything out and the reserve opened cleanly. It was a rare occurrence. I was unlucky, but lucky.

-CHAPTER SEVEN-

YOU DON'T HAVE TO BE MAD TO WORK HERE BUT IT HELPS

THE INVISIBLE BIKE

In 3 Para there were a few old sweats that had never made it past Corporal despite completing 22 years' service. A couple of them were just bitter and twisted old gits, that had given up trying and lived off a legacy of self-proclaimed notoriety or reputation, but most were good blokes that had either been "naughty boys" in their past or had deliberately avoided promotion so they could enjoy their lifestyle without too much responsibility. One of these blokes was a Falklands veteran called "Shuggy," who, as legend went, was a Prince in his home country in West Africa. He had loads of funny stories that he would tell while out for a drink. Once he told me a story about a 3 Para soldier that he'd known back in the day who was medically discharged for being mad. I can't remember his name, so I'll call him Private Smith: Private Smith took his bicycle everywhere with him, pushing it around camp by the handlebars, weaving it in and out of people and obstacles, carrying it up flights of stairs, and leaning it up against walls or fences when he went inside. The problem was, he didn't own a bike! It was an imaginary bike that only he could see. This behaviour was noticed by his superiors and identified as strange, so he was ordered to visit the Medical Centre to speak with a doctor. Smith attended the appointment, entering the Med Centre after securing his bike outside and was promptly referred to the Mental Health department. Within a couple of months, the soldier was awarded a Medical Discharge and on his last day made his way to the C. O's office for his final interview. Walking through camp to Battalion Headquarters, he pushed his bike alongside him before resting it against a wall outside and presenting himself to the Regimental Sergeant Major, who gave him a quick inspection to ensure he was suitably dressed for the occasion. After a few instructions, the RSM marched Smith into the C. O's office where he was thanked for his service, wished good luck, and dispatched to his new life as a civilian. Exiting the office Smith shook hands with the RSM and left, followed by the RSM who saw him out. Stepping outside he strode off purposefully towards his new life when the RSM realised he hadn't collected his bike.

"Smith!" He called.

Smith stopped and turned. "Yes Sir?" he said.

The RSM pointed at the wall. "What about your bike?" he asked.

"What fucking bike?" Smith replied before turning and continuing his exit.

Back then when you joined the army you signed up for a set period. You could opt for periods between 3-22 years and those on longer contracts were rewarded with a higher pay scale. Leaving early could be very difficult for those who had a change of heart, but one way to get out was by a disciplinary or medical discharge. Shuggy didn't know if Smith had been pretending the whole time in an elaborate plan to get himself discharged or whether he was genuinely hallucinating. Apparently, some people thought the bike symbolised his problems and leaving the army enabled him to ditch them and move on.

An Actual Invisible Bike

BARKING MAD

In 1996 during one of our trips to Norway, the kids T.V show Blue Peter sent one of their presenters to film a piece about Arctic survival. The presenter came across a bit full of himself to me and I took an immediate dislike to him, but fortunately my only interaction with him was when he pushed through a few blokes and I snapped. "Say excuse me you fucking prick!" I was a horrible little fucker really.

One of my friends called "Shep" also didn't like him, but he had a reason. Shep had been partnered up with the presenter to dig a snow cave and it had started quite well, with the cameraman getting some footage of them both digging and shovelling. However, as soon as those shots were complete, Shep quickly found himself on his own and assumed the T.V star had gone. Almost finished, Shep completed digging out the tunnel that connected the cave to the outside and went to get a well-earned brew, returning a few minutes later to find that the tunnel had been blocked up with snow and the cameraman was back. As he watched, the presenter, who had also reappeared, rose from the tunnel, shoving the snow out of his way in an over-exaggerated show of effort. Making out he'd done the work he breathlessly spoke into the camera to describe the hard work he'd done before walking off to the warmth of a vehicle again. Shep was a nice bloke from Up North who drank Guinness, rode a Harley Davidson motorbike, and got on with everyone, but even though he laughed about it, I could tell he was snapping.

I watched the Blue Peter footage on YouTube to remind myself of that trip while writing this, and it was great to see some old faces from that time in my career. Among those faces were a few very close friends including some who are still serving now, 25 years later. Unfortunately, there were also a couple who have died, one called Noah who was killed by an IED in Iraq in 2006 and another called Jon, who I was with when we ran away from the elephants in Kenya. Jon was also killed in Iraq in November 2006.

Sometime after returning to the UK another soldier from that footage suffered a mental health meltdown after convincing himself he was to blame for the Dunblane Primary School Massacre. This horrific incident in Scotland, resulted in the deaths of sixteen children and a teacher and the soldier somehow concluded that he was to blame. He reasoned that the cowardly attacker had been triggered into his crazed rampage after seeing him on the television. Lance Corporal Joe's breakdown occurred in the Company Office and had started during a normal conversation with the Company Clerk while sorting out some admin. The clerk was an abrasive Lance Corporal called Paddy who hadn't quite got used to working with paratroopers. I don't know where he'd been posted before, but he should have been warned of the contempt he would be held in by Parachute Regiment soldiers until he had proven himself. That day in his office Paddy was talking to Joe about the tragedy of Dunblane when Joe told him of his guilt.

"It's my fault!" he said. If I hadn't been on the T.V it would never have happened.

Paddy responded dismissively. "How could that be your fault? It's got nothing to do with you!"

Joe was adamant. "It's my fault those kids are dead, he saw me on the T.V and that's why he killed them!"

Paddy probably didn't realise the seriousness of the situation. "Joe don't be stupid, that's ridiculous! He probably didn't even watch Blue Peter you silly bastard."

Joe lost the plot at that point. "It's my fault!" he shouted. "Those kids are dead, and it's my fucking fault!" He rushed over to paddy and grabbed him by the throat with both hands, shaking him violently as he screamed. "They're dead because of me!"

Hearing the shouting the Company Sergeant Major stormed out of his adjoining office.

"What the fuck is going on out here?" He yelled as he swung his door open to be faced by his clerk being throttled by an enraged paratrooper. The scene in front of him immediately changed his approach. An Excellent Sergeant Major who was respected by the blokes and knew his soldiers well, he remained calm, but authoritative.

"Joe, let him go, now!" He ordered.

Joe released his grip immediately.

"Everybody calm fucking down!" the Sergeant Major said, realising that this was not normal behaviour from Joe.

At that point, Joe dropped to his hands and knees and started barking like a dog.

" Woof, woof, woof."

The clerk and the Sergeant Major watched in stunned silence before the Sergeant Major spoke. "Joe!" He commanded. "Stop what you are doing!

Joe reacted immediately and the Sergeant Major carried on. "Stand up and take yourself over to the Med Centre now!"

Joe stood up and did as he was told, leaving the Company Office, and heading for the Medical Centre, which was located directly opposite our Company Office, on the other side of the road.

The second he left, the Sergeant Major grabbed the telephone and called the Reception Desk at the Med Centre and told them what had happened.

We didn't see Joe for a while after that. We all assumed he'd been sent away for psychiatric treatment. The funny thing was, that episode didn't impede his career. He got promoted to full Corporal at the next promotion board! To be fair, he well deserved it, he was an excellent soldier. He'd just had a bit of a "wobble." In the Parachute Regiment, being a bit unhinged can be advantageous, and rightly so!

From then on, he was known as "Mad Joe," but not to his face.

NINJA PLATOON

During my first few years in the Army, we got to do a lot of overseas exercises, with stuff going on every year. In 1994 there was a Battalion exercise in Kenya which everyone did, plus the three Rifle Company's had their own separate trips too, travelling to Botswana, Jamaica, and the U.S.A. These trips would always be eventful, but in a time before mobile phones and social media, snippets of information and rumours would teasingly filter back to those who remained in the U.K. I heard a few good stories come back from the U.S, but my favourite is about an old friend of mine called Luke, who ended a debate with a U.S Navy SEAL in spectacular fashion. Apparently, during a night of drinking at a bar, there had been prolonged banter between the Brits and Americans who were drinking in a bar, about who was the best, who's training was harder etc etc. One of the SEAL's who was carrying a revolver on a hip holster was boasting to Luke that to be in his unit you needed to be crazy, because the training was so horrendous, no sane person would put themselves through the torture. Luke nodded, contemplating the idea, then pointed to the pistol on the Americans side.

"Can I take a look at that?" he asked.

The SEAL looked down at the weapon, then back to Luke. "Sure." He said, withdrawing it and passing it across.

Luke inspected the revolver, feeling the weight in each hand and appreciating the craftmanship before emptying the six rounds from the cylinder onto a table.

"You think you're crazy, do you?" he said, looking the soldier straight in the eye as he replaced one of the rounds into the cylinder. "We'll see about that." He spun the cylinder fast, snapping it shut while it still turned and quickly put the barrel against his own head. Before the American had time to react, Luke pulled the trigger, still looking at him expressionless. The hammer made an audible click as it struck against an empty chamber and Luke passed the pistol back to its owner. "Your turn!" he said.

The SEAL was shocked. "You are fucking crazy man! Why would you do that? He shouted. Collecting his bullets, he promptly left.

Final score: Paras-1, SEALs- 0

Another one of the blokes was asked by an American what the badge on some of the Brits arms was for, that had two crossed swords below a crown. The Physical Training Instructor badge is worn on the right arm, below the parachute wings, but he opted to give an alternative, more impressive answer.

"That's our Ninja Platoon." He answered dryly.

"What?" the shocked soldier replied. "What do you mean, Ninja Platoon?"

The blokes had already realised that their American hosts were extremely polite and agreeable, so he carried on. "In our Regiment, each Battalion has a Platoon of Ninjas." To back up the story he embellished the claim with details on how the Paras sent selected soldiers away, to complete a lengthy Ninja training course in Japan, and somehow, he was believed. The American called over one of his friends and shouted excitedly. "Hey man, have you heard this? These guys have got their own fuckin' Ninjas!"

SHITTO MAN

Exercise Pond Jump West was a six-week training exercise in Canada, based out of a town Called Wainwright, and at the end of the training we had a Battalion social. The entertainment was to be skits, with every Platoon allocated a time slot to perform theirs. These skits were an opportunity for a bit of light entertainment where the Private soldiers would often take the mickey out of their superiors or each other. The day of the party, all the Privates in my Platoon had started drinking at lunchtime because someone opened a crate of beer and although we had intended to do something, the alcohol took over and we all sacked it. By the time the party started that evening, we were already well oiled when "JJ" our Platoon Sergeant, came to tell us we were on in 30 minutes.

"Are you all set?" he asked.

"No, we're not doing one." One of the braver soldiers answered, knowing JJ would be displeased.

"You fucking well are!" he replied. Every Platoon is doing one.

"Yes, but we've been on the piss all day and haven't prepped anything." The soldier explained.

JJ was a mega bloke, but everyone knew not to cross him. He was a big barrel-chested Scotsman with a voice that could be heard on Mars and nobody messed with him.

"You fuckers are doing it!" he said sternly. "I Don't give a shit how much you've drunk! You've got thirty minutes!"

"I'll do it." Said Dave unexpectedly. We all turned to look at him as he continued "But I'll need two people to help me." Scotty and Si Hovey volunteered straight away and sat next to him for instructions. Dave gave his orders. "I need a step ladder, a megaphone, a blanket and a plastic bag." He demanded randomly.

Rather than surprised we were more intrigued at his request; he was renowned for his outlandish behaviour and was one of the Battalions real characters. Dave, Scotty, and Si disappeared, and we didn't see them again until the show started. In the meantime, word got round that Dave was doing a performance and everyone was excited to see what would happen. Half an hour later it was announced that it was the turn of the Signals Platoon and everyone stopped what they were doing to watch. A few seconds of silence built up some tension in the atmosphere, then Scotty burst on stage with a megaphone held to his mouth. Sweeping from side to side as he spoke to the entire audience, he began the show like an enthusiastic boxing ring announcer. "They seek him here….. They seek him there…. They seek him everywhere! …… His name is………Shiiittttto Maaaaan!"

Everyone cheered at the announcement and we were at the edge of our seats as Dave walked on stage wrapped in a blanket. With only his feet visible, he tiptoed to the front of the elevated platform with his head tucked down and the blanket pulled tightly around his shoulders before stopping with his back to us. Spinning around, he dramatically extended one arm fully, opening the blanket on one side like a cape, then did the other side. As he twirled, we caught a glimpse of his face and saw that he was also wearing a mask over his eyes, like the one worn by the Lone Ranger or Zorro. I think the mask was also made from a piece of the blanket and tied off behind his head. The next person on stage was Si who sprinted out with a step ladder held above his head, already opened out and locked in position. He put the ladder down firmly on the stage and held it steady while Dave quickly ascended the steps all the way to the top, and squatted on the two top rungs, still wrapped in his improvised cloak. Si then pulled a clear plastic bag from his pocket, ducked under the ladder, and held it open beneath Dave. In the audience there were mixed emotions, largely influenced by rank and responsibility. At the lower end, where we were, as Privates and Corporals there was excitement, at the Sergeant level there was probably anxiety, and at the Officer level, dread. When Dave's turd dropped into the bag, expertly caught by Si, a new emotional state arose; Disgust! A few local people such as the town Mayor and the pretty ladies from the dentists had been invited along as a way of saying thank you for their support, and someone had even brought their children along. They left the party in utter shock right there and then, just as Si was running around, holding the bag aloft like some kind of championship trophy, presenting it stage left, centre, and stage right. I'll never forget the look on his face because he looked so proud and pleased with himself, obviously encouraged by the rapturous response. Most of the crowd was on its feet, cheering, clapping, laughing, and then chanting "Shitto Man, Shitto Man." The reaction was emphatic, like when a football team scores a winning goal in the final minute of a game. None of us saw that coming, but none of us will ever forget it either.

Shitto Man only made one more appearance after that. It was Dave's last night out before leaving the army and we were in a pub in Dover town centre. Everyone had been buying him drinks and saying their farewells and Dave stood on the Pool table to give a short leaving speech. When he finished someone started to shout, quickly joined by everyone else. "Shitto Man! Shitto Man! Shitto Man! Within a few repetitions it was a loud raucous chant, with all eyes looking to Dave expectantly. At first, he tried to resist, even he knew it wasn't politically correct to take a crap in the middle of a pub, but the chants got louder, and he capitulated. Placing a pint glass on the centre spot, he crouched on the pool table and pointed to the crowd dramatically.

"What do you want?" he shouted, in a deep lingering voice.

The crowd replied excitedly. Shit!"

"When do you want it?" he teased.

"Now!!" everyone screamed.

Standing up, with the pint glass between his feet, Dave pulled down his trousers and squatted over it, right in the middle of that pub. Despite his best efforts, he was unable to perform that night and the glass remained empty as he stood back up and apologised sincerely to his fans. The blokes were very understanding though, and everyone just carried on what they were doing. Must have been stage fright.

GENTLEMEN NEVER TELL

Before departing a young lady's house after a one-night stand, some of the blokes used to grab a souvenir. I once liberated an ABBA Greatest Hits CD from a house in Dover, but other people were much more advanced than me. One of the blokes, Dave (Shitto Man) was once compromised while sneaking out of a back door with a microwave oven. The girl caught him red-handed as he had one foot out the door.

"What are you doing with my microwave?" she demanded to know.

Dave stepped back inside. "I was going to fix it for you." He bluffed unconvincingly, gently placing it back on the kitchen work top.

"It's not fucking broken!" she yelled. "Get out of my house before I call the police!"

He walked out of the house and off the property, then ran all the way back to camp in case she did call the cops. Other regular items to get taken were bras, knickers, and DVD's.

Another old favourite was for a bloke to leave something behind after bedding a married woman. You'd hear tales of Parachute Regiment stickers being stuck under the toilet seat or behind headboards on beds as well as messages written on the back of pictures or inside wardrobes. I remember one bloke telling me that he'd slept with the wife of a soldier from another Regiment whose battalion was on exercise for 3 months in Norway. He'd taken a framed picture off the wall and written "3 Para were here with your Mrs while you were in Norway." He guessed the next time that picture would be taken down was when the soldier got posted and moved to a new house, and he knew the unit was moving six months later.

-PSYCHOTHERAPY-

Boy Vs Man

One of my earliest memories is witnessing my brother being thrown against the wall above his bed by an angry, out of control man who was high on drugs. I can still see it now, my big brother upside down, facing me as his body hit the wall before landing on his bed in a crumpled heap. I was trying to stop the psycho, but at around six years old could do nothing. I was crying and screaming for this monster to leave my brother alone, punching him in the leg. He'd already beat up our mum. Why was he doing this to my brother? The answer was, because my brother had tried to stop this piece of shit attacking our mum. We had both ran into the Living Room after hearing her desperate cries as he assaulted her again. It wasn't the first time, we had heard it before, and we had intervened before, but little boys can't fight grown men, no matter how hard they try. When we were that age, my brother was my hero, he didn't give a fuck about his own safety, to me he was hard as nails, the man of the house, and he would do whatever he could to protect me and our mum, at least that's how I saw him. He was about 8 years old and prepared to fight a grown man, but that is a lot of pressure on a young boys' shoulders, a burden that no child should ever endure. That is the responsibility of the parents. In the first instance my mum should not have gotten involved with this idiot and invited him into our lives, but she did, and by the time he became violent it was too late. He had a hold over her and she was terrified of him. Secondly, there should have been a real man there to defend us, whether that be a neighbour who could hear the screaming or my father who knew the situation. My mums' best friend at that time was our next-door neighbour and her boyfriend was an ex-army bloke who everyone seemed to really respect. He was big, strong, and looked like a tough guy, but looking back now, I think he was a coward. Imagine listening to a woman getting beat up in the house next door and doing nothing. Fuck that!

This vivid image of my brother being thrown resurfaced during a consultation with my psychologist, but I had to admit that I wasn't sure if it was a memory of an event or a memory of a nightmare. It had always seemed real, but under scrutiny I began to doubt it was. I still don't know for sure. One of my psychologists, a great doctor called Dr. Brewster told me that it doesn't matter if the recollection is real. What is important is that you remember it as real, and I did, and still do.

-CHAPTER EIGHT-

DON'T THREATEN PARATROOPERS

MURDER ON THE DANCEFLOOR

Nu-Age nightclub in Dover was the favoured venue for 3 Para blokes to finish the night in. It was cheap to get in, had three different bar areas, and whether you were on a mission to get into a fight, or into a girl's knickers, the chances of success were high. I was out with my mate Matt and his wife Jo, who I also got on well with, and had just re-entered the left-hand upstairs bar after popping to the gents. As I approached, I saw that Jo was standing alone and waving me forwards urgently. As soon as I reached her, she shouted over the noise of the music. "Steve, help Matt!" Pointing to a man on the opposite side of the club she continued. "That wanker over there in the yellow jacket came to my pub and said he was going to stab him in the back when you all got back from Northern Ireland!"

I handed her my pint. "Hold this!" I said and made an immediate bee line for the tall man in the unmistakeable yellow puffer jacket. Matt had taken the slightly longer route to avoid the crowded dancefloor, but in my haste, I just barged my way through, arriving a split second before him and punched the bloke straight in the head. Falling backwards the man landed on his back on a table and I quickly stepped over him, one leg either side. Grabbing his jacket lapels with both hands I pulled him upwards as he tried to get back up, driving my forehead into his face as he lifted. At that point I was grabbed from behind by the head doorman who pulled me backwards and as the yellow jacket got to his feet, he was met by Matt, who gave him a solid left hook to the face and dropped him again before he too was restrained by the bouncers. I relaxed and spoke to the doorman.

"It's over mate, you can let me go, I'm finished with that prick."
I said. I'd spoken to the bouncer on several occasions before and
we got on well, so he gave me the benefit of the doubt and let me
go. I managed to get one more punch in before getting pounced
on again and escorted to the exit. At the door I appealed to the
better nature of the door staff and explained what Matts wife
had told me, and we were allowed to stay, with the other bloke
getting thrown out instead, rounding off a bad night for him.
When I went back upstairs, I went into the right-hand bar to buy
a new drink and a girl came and stood next to me while I waited
to order. "I liked watching you fight just now." She said. Half
an hour later Matt had cleared it with his wife, and I took that
classy young lady back to their spare room on the married quarters, where we spent the night discussing 17th century poetry
and the socio-economic impact of the Berlin Wall collapse. In
the morning Matt and I sneaked out and left it to Jo to get rid of
her. Sometime later, Matt divorced Jo after learning she'd been
unfaithful to him with some men who drank in the pub she
worked at, coincidentally the same pub the bloke in the yellow
jacket used.

THE BLOODWORTH
BLOODBATH

When we moved to Dover from Aldershot in 1995 our reputation had preceded us, and before we even got there, we were told the Town Council had failed in a bid to prevent us from coming. A few of the pubs had even banned us, with a couple displaying signs at the door saying, "out of bounds to airborne troops," apparently some of the locals thought 600 paratroopers getting drunk in their town was a bad idea. Previous army units had been known to cause trouble and vandalise property, and the assumption was that we would be even worse, because of our reputation for aggression and general lunacy. Among the people displeased with our arrival were the local self-appointed tough guys that frequented the pubs and clubs and the large amount of bootleggers that used the Dover to Calais ferries to buy copious amounts of cigarettes and alcohol to sell at a massive profit. It took a while, but eventually our reputation got better and better when people started to realise that the blokes were actually decent people as long as you left them alone. Within a couple of months our blokes had fought and battered just about every scumbag in town, usually on a Friday or Saturday night, and usually either in a nightclub called Nu-Age or the Charcoal Grill kebab shop. The bouncers who worked in the clubs soon realised that bullying paratroopers or getting punchy with them when splitting up fights was not going to work, and many found themselves on the wrong end of a beating when they tried. The only people who can stop the blokes fighting are other paratroopers who they respect or fear. Quite quickly all the doormen were 3 Para soldiers and some of them were absolutely nails. I saw one of them, called Goldie knock a bloke out with a little slap round the head once.

One night I was on Guard Duty when the Guard Commander, a Corporal came into the rest area where we were watching a DVD. "I need three blokes to come with me into town. It's kicking off!" He said sharply.
I was straight up and out the door with two of the others, and we jumped in the back of the Land Rover parked outside. In the passenger seat was the Battalion Orderly Sergeant (BOS) but he was not Para Reg, he was a Clerk, and he looked very nervous when we got to town and saw a small crowd outside the kebab shop.
"What shall we do?" He asked the Corporal.
"You wait here, we'll deal with this!" He was told.
Jumping over the tailgate we followed the Corporal towards the Charcoal Grill to see what was going on. In a shop doorway next to the kebab shop was a bloke I knew from my old platoon in A Company. He was another Steve B. There were three Steve B's in that single platoon, but he was known as "Taff." Having ripped his top off in a drunken rage Taff Bloodworth stood there with his fists clenched, shouting out loud.
"Fucking 3 Para are here now, and we run this fucking town you civvy twats!"
In front of Taff, across the road were several agitated men and women shouting back at him, the women were especially loud and aggressive. One of the men moved towards Taff with his chest puffed out and arms out to the side. "Come on then!" He screamed, pulling his fist back like he was cocking a weapon. The instant he was in striking range there was an audible thud as Taff intercepted his punch with one of his own, a crushing right hand that dropped him like a sack of spuds. As soon as he hit the floor, another paratrooper appeared from nowhere and quickly dragged the casualty away, punching him in the head as he did so until he went limp. Seeing his friend get knocked out like that encouraged another man to step forward and he got the same treatment, this time a devastating left hook from Taff

with additional punches from a different soldier who lurked in the shadows. Paratroopers are like Velociraptors and will fight as a pack if attacked, without hesitation. Right or wrong, the blokes stick together, sometimes water is thicker than blood.

We had arrived just in time to see this and as I got to the scene a woman shouted at me desperately.

"Fucking stop him! You've got to stop him!" I think one of the unconscious men was her boyfriend and another from the group was making his way across the road to defend their honour. I just laughed at her and said. "You try and stop him!" Taff was a great guy who didn't look for trouble, he'd actually looked out for me when I was a new bloke and kept me out of trouble. They'd started on the wrong man, he was going berserk, and the third man fared no better than his mates, doing a good impression of a punchbag. Suddenly the sound of police sirens echoed down the street and we ran across the road.

"Taff, you need to get the fuck out of here mate!" I said. "Come get in the Rover and we'll take you back to camp!" Two of us grabbed him by the arms and pulled him away from the scene, and as we ran back to the wagon, the flashing blue lights of the police car reflected off the walls and the siren got louder. One of the blokes jumped straight into the back and we all helped Taff climb in before jumping in behind him and pulling down the rear door flap.

"Stay low and stay still Taff!" The Guard Commander instructed. The BOS was still sitting in the front seat nervously. "Who is that?" He asked.

"It's no one." Replied the Corporal as he sat in the driver's seat. "We're going back now."

Before the engine even started the back flap suddenly lifted and we were faced by a tall, uniformed Police Officer. "Hello gents, what are you up to?" He said casually. 3 Para sent patrols into town regularly to build relationships with the pub landlords and conduct low level self-policing, so it wasn't unusual for us to be there.

"Nothing much, just heading back to camp." We replied innocently.

The officer looked down at Taff who lay on the floor in the foetal position like the world's worst hide-and-seeker. "And who might that be?" he quizzed. It was pretty obvious, and the civvies had probably told him what just happened. Plus, Taff was half naked with blood on his face and knuckles.

"We're just giving him a lift." We answered.

The copper looked at us and nodded unconvincingly. "Is that right? Get him out of here!" He ordered, pointing up towards the barracks at the top of the hill. He knew exactly who it was, but he probably appreciated the rough justice that had just been dealt to some low life's.

CHOOSE YOUR ENEMIES
AND DON'T CHOOSE US

As a young Private soldier I was a real product of the training system I'd undergone. I didn't like civilians, had no respect for soldiers from other Regiments, and loved being part of the Airborne Brotherhood where I was surrounded by likeminded individuals. Anyone who questioned or undermined the status of my unit or brethren would quickly get my blood boiling. One time this happened was during a bit of down-time in Canada while a bunch of us were enjoying a few cold beers in an outdoor seating area. A Corporal, who was an army clerk had been talking to some of the others, and as I walked past his table I overheard him gobbing off. They were good lads that had only been in Battalion a couple of months and he was taking advantage of their naivety.

Posturing like a Peacock he laid down the law. "You lot are just a bunch of fucking Joe Crows and I'm a Corporal, who's spent more time in the NAAFI queue than you've spent in Battalion. Now, which one of you wants to buy me a beer?"

Without breaking my stride I turned around, walked the couple of paces to where he was sat and grabbed him tightly by the throat with my right hand. His eyes nearly popped out of his head as I squeezed his windpipe and pushed him sideways onto the table. Pinning him to the plastic table, flat on his back, I stood over him and snarled angrily. "You are a fucking Hat! You do not speak to paratroopers like that! Do it again and I'll knock your fucking teeth out of your head!" I looked at the blokes who were also a bit shocked because I'm normally pretty quiet. "Lads, we are paratroopers, we do not let anybody talk to us like c**ts! Ever!" I looked back at the clerk who was bright red, with veins bulging in his head.

"Sorry Steve." He croaked, with minimum oxygen.

I let him go and sat back down with my own mates who weren't shocked at all. They knew what I was like.

Another time I lost my temper over someone being disrespectful was during a visit to an RAF base. The pub on base hosted a party every Wednesday night, and me and a bloke called Buck were leaving at about 0100hrs when he got into an argument with another group of blokes. In the chaos of the place closing I hadn't even realised, but as we walked away from the venue he was very agitated and told me there had been a bit of pushing and shoving, and that one of the men had called him a "stupid para prick." At that point I turned around and headed back towards the pub. "We can't have that mate!" I stated, shaking my head. "Can't let that one go unanswered!"

Buck identified the group of three men as they walked away with their backs to us. "That's them." He said.

There were a lot of people around, so I followed them through the camp and watched them enter an accommodation block through a fire exit next to the footpath. A few seconds after, we were also in the building, and I saw them through the glass panel of another door as they went into their individual rooms. Bursting through that door with Buck close behind me I began to rant. "You fuckers think you can gob off to Para Reg?! Gob off now you fucking pussies!"

The closest one was in the doorway of a room on the left-hand side of the corridor and stood his ground.

"You can't come in here, fuck off!" he ordered, pointing back towards the door. The room doors were staggered and alternated left and right, so I marched down the corridor and punched him in the face with a straight left, sending him sprawling into his room. The other two began protesting loudly so I continued forward, not even stopping as I punched the second one with a right and then the third with another left. Buck was still stood where we'd entered and I turned around to face him as the third man stood up, punching him once more, this time with my right hand for equality and diversity. I walked past Buck, "let's go" I said, and we exited through the fire door, breaking into a run in case the police had been called. Buck was really excited.

"I have never seen anything like that mate!" he kept saying. "That was fucking awesome!"

"Para Reg mate. Nobody talks to us like that!" I told him.

The following morning Buck was still over-excited about the incident and talked about it to some of the others as we ate breakfast in the cookhouse. As he talked I noticed a group of RAF firefighters come in through the door. They'd come in every mealtime, dressed in their big fire retardant boots and trousers, with braces and matching t-shirts that had "FIRE" written on the back. I never knew why they felt the need to do that, there was probably a higher likelihood of a Taliban attack than a fire, and we weren't cutting about in our body armour and helmets. I recognised one of the firemen straight away, although he had sprouted a black eye since I'd last seen him. Another one had a cut and swelling on his mouth and I lowered my head to avoid eye contact. Discretely, I informed Buck that they were there, and we made a quick exit.

BLACK AND BLUE BY
THE BOYS IN BLUE

When one of the blokes was jumped and beaten up by a group of men one night, I decided in my drunken state to avenge him. Knowing only that there were three of them, and they were Northerners, I went looking for them with a mate from Battalion called Gypsy Jim. It was about 0230hrs so there weren't that many people about and when we saw three men walking towards us on the opposite side of the road I shouted out. "Oi, did you fuckers jump one of our blokes earlier?"

One of them shouted back in a deep northern accent. "Mind your own fucking business, unless you want to get jumped yourself!"

At the time, that response, in that accent, seemed conclusive evidence that it was indeed them, so Jim and I crossed the road to confront them. Without saying another word, I walked up to the bloke in the middle and headbutted him in the face, sending him reeling backwards. To be fair, I'd overestimated my head-butting skills and was surprised he was still standing. Not only was he standing, but he put his fists up and started bouncing on his toes in a boxing stance. A trickle of blood ran from his left nostril as he started to bob and weave.

"Ya bastard! Come on then, I'll fucking kill ya!" he shouted angrily. The way he was moving told me he could fight, so I also adopted a fighting position and we faced off, him in an orthodox and me in a southpaw stance. I thought it was important to hit first so I threw the fastest punch I knew, a backfist, which connected and caused a trickle of blood to come from his other nostril. I saw the comedy value even in that moment and was rather

161

pleased with myself to be honest, but although fast, the punch had little power behind it and I think he was more insulted than hurt.

"Ya bastard, ya think you're fast?" he said. "Ya think you're fucking fast?"

To add insult to injury, I hit him with another backfist, but this time followed it up with real punches as he fought back, both connecting with each other's heads. Jim was engaged in his own fight with one of the others, but the third bloke went for me, punching me in the left side of the head. Even though I hadn't practiced martial arts for several years, I instinctively spun clockwise and did a spinning kick to his body that sent him backwards, creating a bit of space for me. I then executed a one-step sidekick to the leg of the first opponent in an effort to disable him but missed the knee and caught his thigh. This made him even angrier, and he started shouting again. "Ya trying to break my leg ya bastard? I'll kill ya!"

Suddenly Jim was sat on the floor with the other two trying to kick him so I ran across and booted one of them so he could get up, and we carried on scrapping until the police arrived in a car and a riot van to split us up. As soon as the police arrived, we all stopped fighting and complied with their orders, except for the bloke I'd hit first who was going ballistic, still enraged that I'd hit him and screaming at the police. After a couple of minutes, to calm him down, he was put into the cage in the back of the van, while the rest of us were split up so the police could ask us questions. Jim and I were told to sit in the police van on the seats while the officers had a chat with each other outside. The Northerner was still gobbing off, saying he was going to press charges and find out where I lived etc. etc.

"It's finished!" I said. "We had a fight. Get over it and keep your mouth shut!"

One of the policemen came in and sat with me and Jim to get our details and was writing them down in his notebook when a policewoman opened the side door. Holding an extended telescopic baton in one hand she banged it on the van floor several times until it collapsed before handing it to the officer talking to me then left.

"I shouldn't have hit you with this, I read the situation wrong, and I admit that." He said.

I had no idea what he was talking about. "Wasn't me mate, you never hit me." I replied.

The copper insisted. "Listen, I'm admitting I was wrong to hit you. I've got the paperwork here and I can take your statement right now. I'd rather do that and get it over and done win6th."

"It must have been someone else mate." I persisted. "You didn't hit me."

Jim interjected. "Steve, he hit you round the head with his baton mate!"

I looked at him a little confused. "Did he? When?" I queried.

"When you and that bell end were scrapping!" Jim said, pointing at the bloke locked up in the back.

The policeman was looking at me in disbelief, I think he was surprised at the ineffectiveness of his weapon, and he was obviously worried I'd press charges or make a complaint against him.

"Mate, thanks for your honesty, but I can't even remember it, so I'm not bothered. I just want to go back to camp." I told him. I was the instigator, and I just wanted to get out of there, any further investigation would only highlight my guilt. The policeman left the vehicle and closed the door behind him. I turned to the bloke in the back who was still protesting loudly. "Oi, shut the fuck up and we can all go home you prick! You're just making things worse!"

The only person to get arrested that night was the bloke who wouldn't calm down and he was taken to Folkestone to spend the rest of the night in a cell. Jim and I were given a lift back to camp.

The next day at brunch in the Cookhouse I saw Jim again. We both had hangovers nut I also had a big bruise on the side of my head and behind the ear. My ear itself was black and blue from the baton strike. I also had a deep cut on my chin from an uppercut I got hit with. Jim was telling the others about our fight and calling me Jean-Claude Van Brown because of the kickboxing. I bet it wasn't anywhere near as impressive as he remembered it, we were very drunk.

-CHAPTER NINE-

FOOD AND DRINK

FANCY A BOTTLE OF MILK?

Northern Ireland was a mental place. I only did one tour there in 1997 and that was cut short from the planned six-months to just four because of the recently imposed peace process. We were in West Belfast where the dynamics could change drastically from one road to the next. Some nationalist areas painted their kerbstones in the colours of the Irish flag, alternating in green, white, and orange, and proudly displayed huge murals painted on walls, dedicated to imprisoned or martyred members of republican paramilitary groups. In these places the hatred was palpable, and the inhabitants made their loyalties clear, throwing the occasional missile at you such as a bottle, brick, or in one case, a bicycle. In contrast, you could literally turn a corner and enter a street of red, white, and blue kerbs, union flags, loyalist murals and a community that treated you with indifference or sometimes even waved hello. One evening I was on a foot patrol on an estate called the Ardoyne. This was a staunch republican area where tricolour flags flew and soldiers were despised, even the dogs were trained to hate us and would often go crazy in the gardens as we patrolled past. We'd been out for a while and were on our way back to camp when a small kid approached me. The young boy had been standing outside a house with a couple of adults who watched on as he walked towards me holding an empty glass milk bottle with both hands. He must have only been four years old. He stopped and turned to look at the two men who waved him on deviously. It was obvious what he'd been told to do, and we could all see it coming. A captain who was in charge called out to me. "Don't hit him Brown! Do not hit him!" He ordered.
I switched my gaze to the officer quickly and shook my head in

disbelief. Did that moron actually think I would strike a little kid who was just doing as he was told by some scumbags? That kid came right up to me and I stopped still. "Hello mate, are you alright?" I asked. The kid did not reply and instead I watched as he threw that bottle at me as hard as he could. It barely made it halfway up my leg with zero impact before smashing on the floor at my feet, much to the entertainment of the two idiots. All I could do was shake my head and carry on. "See ya mate." I said. I bet he turned out to be a right little shit!

A Loyalist mural and a Nationalist mural in N.I

HOW ABOUT A NICE GLASS OF BEER?

One Sunday morning I was woken up by the sound of someone shouting in the accommodation block. Bleary eyed after a heavy night of drinking, I got up, wearing just a pair of boxer shorts and opened my bunk door to see a young Private walking through the corridor in uniform calling my name. The only people who wore uniform at the weekend were the blokes on guard duty, so I guessed he'd been sent from the Guardroom. I knew everyone in 3 Para at the time, but didn't recognise him, so he must have been a new bloke.

"What's up mate?" I shouted.

He turned around and started walking back towards me. "Are you Steve Brown?" he asked anxiously.

"Yes mate, what's the matter?" I replied.

He was obviously in a rush and spoke quickly. "The Guard Commander has sent me to come and get your clothes from last night, and anything else you want to get rid of. The police are here to arrest you for assault!"

I had no recollection of fighting the previous night, but I used to get so drunk I'd forget pretty much everything from ten or eleven o'clock onwards on nights out, including fights and sexual experiences. I checked my hands to see if there was any blood on them and pressed my knuckles to see if they were bruised. I was fairly confident I hadn't been scrapping. "It's okay mate, I don't need you to take anything thanks. Where are they now?" I said.

"They're at the Guardroom. The Corporal is delaying them so you can get rid of any evidence." he answered. "They won't be far behind me though."

I left my bunk and went straight to see my mate Scotty who was fast asleep in his bed. Scotty was a nightmare to wake up and he'd often start swinging if you caught him in a deep sleep. You had to wake him up gently, then step back and keep talking to him while he came round, or he'd fall back down and go to sleep again. When he eventually became lucid enough for conversation, I asked him if I had been in a fight. We'd gone out together, so he would know. He said that he'd left the nightclub before me, but I'd come to see him when I got back at about two-thirty in the morning. "No mate, you weren't fighting. You'd have told me if you were because you were in here waffling for ages!" he said sarcastically. He knew I had blackouts when I drank enough Stella Artois, which was every Friday and Saturday night. As I left, I told him the police were looking for me and he just laughed and went back to sleep. Soon afterwards there was a knock at my door, and I opened it to see two, plain clothed policemen stood outside my room.

"Are you Steve Brown?" One of them asked sternly.

"Yes I am. What's the matter?"

They arrested me on suspicion of assault, causing grievous bodily harm, and after placing my clothes and boots from the previous night into a plastic forensics bag, took me away to Dover Police station for questioning. After being processed and spending a short time in a cell I was taken to an interview room for questioning and I was asked about where I'd been, who I'd been with, and what time before they got into it.

"Do you know someone called Joel?" asked the officer.

One of my best mates was called Joe, and I was out with him the night before, but I wasn't going to volunteer that. "No, I don't know anyone called Joel." I said.

"Do you know someone called Michelle?" came the second question.

The penny dropped. "Oh Michelle! Yeah, I know her. You know her history, don't you? She's a nut case!" I exclaimed.

Michelle was a barmaid that I'd had a couple of one-night stands with before finding out she'd accused one of the other blokes of rape. Charges were never pressed because when the police came on camp to arrest him, he was on crutches with two broken legs from a disastrous parachute jump. She'd told the police that he had chased her along the beach, rugby tackle her and raped her, but it was obviously a lie.

"We're not here to discuss that." I was told. "How would you describe your relationship with Michelle?"

"We haven't got a relationship!" I stated. "I've just had sex with her a couple of times."

The policeman referred to his paperwork. "Really?" he said, before reading from her statement. "Because she describes it as a long-term relationship that she recently ended, and you were very upset about."

The truth was, I'd actually told her I didn't want to see her again the previous night, and she was pissed off. Unfortunately, a bloke she was out with had been beaten up, and she made up a story that I'd threatened to hurt him in the club, then attacked him outside, because I was jealous. The police must have doubted her story if they knew her record but questioned me for a long time anyway.

"I see you are wearing a ring on your right hand. For the record, can you describe that ring?" the copper asked.

Like lots of blokes, I wore a gold Regimental ring for years on my right ring-finger. "It's a Parachute Regiment cap-badge ring." I said, holding out my hand to show it.

The officer acknowledged it. "The victim has an indentation in his face that bears a strong resemblance to the design on that ring." He explained.

I had to chuckle at that. I doubted it was true, but the image of it was funny. Imagine walking around with a Para Reg stamp on your face! And imagine how hard you'd have to hit someone to do that!

No charges were placed against me and, after the police's time had been wasted by that psycho once more, I got my clothes and boots back six months later.

After that had all blown over, I bumped into her once more on a night out, and when she started chatting like we were old mates I just went along with it. I couldn't be bothered with any more strife, and she was totally denying that she'd accused me of anything, claiming the police had made it all up. Stood in a quiet area near some stairs I humoured her for a few minutes, waiting for a polite moment to end the conversation and get away, but before I got the chance my good friend Jonah walked past and saw us.

"Why are you talking to her?" he said angrily. "She tried to get you done!" He'd stopped in his tracks, surprised I'd given her my time.

"Mate, I can't be arsed with any more trouble, it's not worth it." I explained.

"Fuck that! She's a slag! Tell her to fuck off!" Jonah said, before turning to walk off.

He wasn't wrong! "You're right." I agreed, then turned back to her. "He's right you know; you are a slag! Fuck off and tell your bullshit to someone else!" I said sharply.

Her response was immediate, and she screamed angrily in a high pitch while smashing a pint glass into the side of my face, causing a few small cuts, but luckily no real damage. I just shook my head in disbelief. "Fuck off!" I repeated.

This time she punched me in the head, she had no glasses left. I was brought up knowing that men should never hit women and wasn't even angry. However, one of my other good friends who didn't share my convictions, had witnessed the whole thing and without warning punched her. She went backwards straight legged, and hit the floor flat on her back, completely unconscious. My mate stepped over her as his momentum took him forwards, then turned to look at me.

"I think I better leave!" he said worriedly.

"I think I better come with you!" I replied, and we left immediately. On the way back to camp he explained how he'd been watching events unfold and couldn't understand why I'd just stood there and not retaliated.

"I don't hit women." I said.

"Neither do I mate!" he replied. "But I'll make an exception if they glass me then fucking punch me!" He was a good bloke. He just couldn't stand to see an airborne brother getting assaulted. He would have intervened no matter who it was. For the next few days, I waited for that knock on the door from the police, convinced that she'd say it was me that hit her, but miraculously it never happened. To be fair she probably couldn't even remember her own name after that. He hit her like a fucking freight train!

I only ever heard about that psycho woman one more time after that. As a Physical Training Instructor, I used to take the platoon fitness most mornings, and we'd always meet up outside the stores at 0800hrs before setting off. One morning, one of the blokes, called Griff, was missing and it transpired he'd gone out for a pint the previous night. After waiting for a couple of minutes we left without him, returning an hour later to find he still hadn't come back. Griff was a binge fitness fanatic, who had immense natural strength and would do a thousand press ups a night when in the mood. Eventually he turned up, late in the morning and I asked him where he'd been for P.T.

"Do you know a bird called Michelle?" he said, with a look of horror.

"Fucking hell, did you shag her last night?" I asked.

Griff told me the story of what had happened. He'd woken up in a strange bed, in an unknown house, to see her standing by her bedroom door, rubbing the end of a cigarette lighter up and down the wall, with sparks flying off it as she stared at him.

"I bet you don't even know my fucking name, do you?" she snapped.

"Er no, I don't actually." he laughed.

Well, I know your name, Griff! And I know your mate's names, Steve, Scotty and Jonah as well!" she shouted angrily.

Griff grabbed his clothes and started to get dressed quickly, and

172

when he stood up to leave, she opened the top drawer of her cabinet and pulled out a hammer.

"You're not going anywhere!" she snapped, wielding the hammer aggressively.

Griff sat down on the bed and talked to his captor, listening to her rant about not being a psycho and how misunderstood she was, until he saw an opportunity to escape and legged it out of the bedroom, down the stairs and out the front door. Finding camp was never that difficult because it was at the top of a big hill, next to a huge castle.

Griff died of a sudden heart attack in 2019 about a year after leaving the army. He was only 42 years old and left behind a wife and fifteen-year-old daughter.

KEBAB SHOP CHIPS

The first time I met an old friend of mine called Mick we got into a fight together in the infamous Charcoal Grill kebab shop in Dover. We'd started drinking early on a Saturday afternoon and both got the munchies sometime in the evening, so decided to get something to eat. While we were waiting for our chips two men and a woman also came in to order and one of the men started talking to Mick. They were Irish, and Mick, an Irishman himself, picked up on their accents and chatted happily. They were all obviously drunk, but one of the men was worse for wear than the others and began acting up. Although he wasn't being overly aggressive, his body language told me he was winding himself up. I had just picked up my parcel of chips from the counter when the stranger spoke.

"You look like John Barnes." He said to Mick. This was nothing new because Mick does look a little bit like the ex-England footballer John Barnes and even sounds a bit like him.

Me and Mick exchanged glances we could both see where this was going.

"Oh yeah? A lot of people have told me that." Mick replied calmly.

"Mind you, all you n**gers look the same!" he spouted nastily.

The kebab shop worker looked at me as I immediately put my chips back on the countertop. "Please, no trouble!" he pleaded, but it was too late, I had way too much respect for Mick to let that one go, and I punched that twat straight in the head. Mick immediately grabbed hold of him and punched him, and they started trading blows violently. I was then hit from behind and began another fight with the second Irishman who was angry that I'd attacked his mate, shouting that I was out of order. In between punching each other I was also shouting at him, saying that nobody called my mate the n-word. On hearing that, my opponent decided his friend had deserved it and we agreed to call it a day, re-entering the Charcoal Grill to split up the other two because someone shouted that the police were coming. When I walked back in Mick was punching the bent-over Irishman with uppercuts to the head and I got between them to stop the fight. As I did that the woman started punching me in the head while screaming "Not two on one! Not two on one!"

I turned towards her and told her. "I'm trying to break it up you silly bitch!" At the same moment she stopped, her boyfriend suddenly stood bolt upright and grabbed me around the throat with both hands, squeezing tight. My instinctive reaction was to headbutt him and I smashed my oversized forehead into his already bloodied face as hard as I could. He let go, but credit where it's due, he stayed on his feet, he was battered, but he was tough. We left that fine establishment and started running when we heard the police sirens. Mick was snapping because of my final headbutt.

"You prick!" he said while we ran down the road. "All I wanted to do was break that fucker's nose, but you had to come in with that massive head and fucking smash it!" We both had blood on our hands and clothes, so we called it a night and went back to camp.

Drawing by my good friend Joe. circa 1996

-PSYCHOTHERAPY-

BAGGY TROUSERS

I watched from behind as a small boy stood alone before a huge stone building looking up in awe. I couldn't see his face, but I could feel he was lonely and nervous.

"How old do you think this little boy is?" Asked Dr Jackson.

He was small, but steady on his feet. "He's about four years old, maybe five." I answered. "He's scared."

"Do you get a sense of who that small boy is?" she said.

There was silence as I concentrated. I wanted to ensure I didn't overthink it or influence my thoughts and just let the scene unfold naturally. "Yes, it's me." I said. "It's me as a little boy."

The building resembled an ancient Egyptian or Mayan tomb and the stones that made up the structure were also laid on the ground, perfectly flat and even. They were a sand colour and although they had a rough surface, were perfectly cut, with neat, straight edges that aligned perfectly. Inside a stone frame was an enormous door made of a dark rustic wood, reinforced with lengths of blackened metal which criss-crossed it at right angles. A loud, rattling, ratcheting noise broke the silence and the door slowly began to rise, the mechanism straining under the huge load. About ten feet up it stopped, and the boy watched apprehensively to see what would come out. A man appeared from the darkness inside and stood in the doorway for a second before beginning to walk towards the boy. The man had a reassuring presence about him and although his face was out of focus and unidentifiable, he was not at all sinister, but peaceful. Dressed in beige trousers and waistcoat with a white shirt and hat he resembled a 1940's archaeologist or the lead character in The Great Gatsby as he reached the boy, stood on his left-hand side and placed his hand gently on his back, between the shoulders compassionately. I was still watching this scene from behind as they both faced the tomb together and my emotions were starting to escalate. A massive wave of relief came over the boy when he felt the hand on his back and when I looked at him again his clothes were suddenly way too big, the trousers crumpled up at his feet. The back of his suit also hung so low it gathered on the floor with the sleeves flopping loosely off his arms and the shoulders barely hanging on to his tiny frame. Up to that point I hadn't even noticed that the boy was wearing a suit. Boys don't wear suits, men do. But now that a man had come along the suit had returned to the size it should have been. "Do you get a sense of who the man is?" Dr Jackson asked.

It was me again. The older me and the young me held hands and walked side by side into the safety of the tomb.

-CHAPTER TEN-

WRONG TIME
WRONG PLACE

GUTS, BUT NO GLORY

A few weeks into our 2006 Afghanistan tour, while on my way to the cookhouse to get a brew one night, I bumped into one of my blokes who was walking in the opposite direction. Nick was our medic; he was extremely keen and capable and always had a smile on his face. As soon as I saw him, I knew something was wrong, he was walking slowly with his head hanging down and looked knackered, like he'd just finished a 10 miler from hell. As he got close, I spoke. "You alright Nick?"
He lifted his head to look at me and even in the dimly lit passage I could see the haunted look on his face. He looked like shit!
"Are you ok mate? You look like shit!" I said subtly. I was genuinely worried about him.
"I feel like shit mate." He replied solemnly. "I'll be alright though; I just need to chill out for a bit and get my head down."
I turned around to walk back with him and as we walked, he told me about what had happened.
Nick had been visiting the cookhouse for a brew when a Toyota Hilux had driven into camp carrying Afghan Army casualties from an I.E.D strike. On arrival they were met by British Army medics and rushed away for emergency treatment, but the mess left behind was horrendous. At the explosion site among the carnage and confusion, casualties were loaded hastily onto the Hilux along with corpses, body parts and internal organs in a bid to salvage as many lives as possible. On his way back Nick had come across the aftermath and noticed a couple of young lads from 3 Para walking past also. 3 Para were in the first few days of their tour with more troops arriving every day and Nick, being a compassionate bloke didn't think it was right for them to see such a horrific scene before they had even been outside

the wire. Selflessly he had fetched some bin bags and cleared up the mess with his bare hands, scooping up pieces of intestine, lumps of flesh and flaps of skin so that others wouldn't have to see it. Another time during that tour Nick would again show his commitment to others when he ran towards an explosion to administer lifesaving first aid to casualties without any regard for his own safety. Great medic, excellent soldier, mega bloke.

TODAY IS THE DAY

Another time where I was really worried about someone's mental health during that 2006 tour in Afghanistan was when I returned from paternity leave and reunited with the blokes who I'd left behind for several weeks. One of the men in my team, Andy, was a really chilled out, softly spoken bloke who was phenomenally fit. The day I went back out to Afghanistan was the last day of his deployment before he was flying home. The blokes had been having a hard time with lots of violent engagements with the enemy and it had taken its toll on everyone, including him. I noticed his mood seemed very sombre and he was quieter than usual, and I'll never forget what he said to me because I thought it was horrendous. He told me that for the last few weeks, every day, he thought he was going to die, that he was going to be killed that day. The way he spoke was different to what I'd heard from anyone before. On tour, I think most soldiers accept that every day they *might* be killed because that is a real, ever present risk that comes with the job and everyone deals with it in their own way. But that is very different from waking up every day truly believing that today is the day you *will* be killed. The way he told me was completely non-emotional and matter of fact but to me it was significant. "Fucking hell mate, it's a good time for you to go home!" I said. Not long after that tour Andy left the Army and joined the Police. I hope he's doing well, cracking bloke.

THEY STARTED IT

In 2001 I was sent to Macedonia with the Pathfinders on the NATO deployment called Operation Essential Harvest, and we worked in the Tetovo Valley area. Some of the villages in our area were ethnic Albanian Muslim and controlled by the Albanian National Liberation Army and some were Macedonian Christian and controlled by Macedonian armed forces. These two groups hated each other and would regularly exchange rifle and machine gun fire across the fields and roads that separated them, always blaming one another for initiating the firefight. Neither group were particularly fond of us either. The Macedonian army thought we were protecting a group of people who were attacking them in their own country and the Albanians thought we were on the side of the Macedonian army. One day we were tasked to determine which side was the aggressor by covertly inserting into one of the villages and waiting to see who fired first. Under the cover of darkness, we sneaked into a building site on the edge of one village and only a few hundred metres from the other and settled down for the night, keeping low and using the walls as cover. Sure enough the shooting started and we could tell immediately what direction it was coming from as machine gun fire rattled directly over our position and we reported back to our HQ. Once we had done that the mission was accomplished, but we couldn't go anywhere until the morning when it all stopped because it went on all night with sporadic bursts whizzing in both directions to our left, right, and straight overhead. That was a strange job that one and not the best sleep I ever had.

On another night during that tour, we received a call that a firefight was ensuing between two other villages that we had visited a few times previously. We were tasked to drive into them and convince them to stop. We had established a relationship with the village leaders and the patrol commander called ahead to tell them we were approaching in three British army Land Rovers and not to shoot. As we approached, we could see the tracer rounds and hear the weapons firing in both directions and we safely entered the village. After a few minutes, our patrol commander calmed the leader down and although the outgoing firing didn't stop it did reduce a lot. We called ahead again to warn off the next village and headed down the road that linked the two. The narrow country lane ran parallel to a series of large farmers' fields that served as no-man's land and as we drove bullets streamed across the open ground to our left at head height only metres away. I remember seeing a bright flash and hearing a loud bang as a projectile was launched from a position ahead. It whooshed across the fields and exploded on impact in the other village. That distance was about half a mile. "What the fuck was that?" I said to my mate who was driving.

"RPG?" he replied.

"It can't be an RPG." I said. "That's about 800 metres, it's too far."

"I bet it's an RPG." He re-stated.

Arriving at the next village we knew there was a checkpoint with a small defensive position made of sandbags and pulled up slowly. The patrol commander got out of the front vehicle and approached the sentry and I also debussed from my vehicle. There was a short exchange of words before the voices suddenly got louder and shouting started. One of the other soldiers had debussed also and we moved forward to see what was going on. There were lots of men shouting from behind the sandbags and our interpreter, a local civilian was trying his best to mediate. He came over to us and said "They say you must put down your weapons. They say you must lie down on the ground."

Fortunately, our patrol commander was a very strong character with a confident, no-nonsense attitude. "They can fuck off!" he said. "That is not happening!" He walked right up to the gate and began shouting at the leader on the other side, with the interpreter doing his best to keep up translating. We were massively outnumbered and outgunned, and the tension was palpable but there was no way we were going to do that, not a chance. We hadn't anticipated this scenario or planned for it, so I told the soldier stood next to me what my intentions were if the shooting started. From previous patrols and map studies I described to him the escape route I would take, and the rendezvous point I would head for and he agreed to do the same. At that point he passed me something. "Here, take this mate." He said.

In the darkness he discretely passed me an item I had never seen before but guessed what it was.

"Is that a Flash-Bang?" I asked quietly.

"Yes mate." He confirmed.

He was a liaison officer from a different unit and had obviously been issued the low explosive "stun grenade" for exactly this kind of situation, but I had never used one before, but it looked like a small version of any other hand grenade.

"Just pull the pin and throw it like a normal grenade yes?" I asked.

"Yes mate." He replied.

"Nice one, thanks." I said. I'd have taken anything to bolster my arsenal at that point. All we had was rifles.

I sidled over to the driver's side of my Land Rover, where the driver sat apprehensively and briefed him on my intentions too. He agreed to do the same as well.

Eventually we were allowed through the checkpoint and entered the village and our patrol commander immediately got to work trying to convince the leader to cease firing. This was not an easy task because incoming fire was still being received from the opposite village. At one point after a burst of machine gun fire rattled past us, the defenders responded with a ferocious wall of fire that I had never experienced before, sending a deafening hail of thousands of bullets back towards their enemy, lighting up the sky with tracer rounds and explosions that lasted for about 30 seconds.

As a soldier I appreciated that, it was impressive, and I looked at my mate laughing. "Fucking hell!" I said. "Get some!"

He was nodding and grinning also.

Despite the huge ammunition expenditure from both sides, I think only one person was shot that night, and it was an innocent child who'd been sheltering inside their home. There is a lot to be said for the Marksmanship Principles taught in the British Army!

During World War Two the German paratroopers had their own version of the Ten Commandments and number five was:

> 5. *"The most precious thing in the presence of the foe is ammunition. He who shoots uselessly, merely to comfort himself, is a man of straw who merits not the title of Paratrooper."*

After a lot of phone calls, accusations, and counter accusations we were able to negotiate a cease fire and it went quiet. When dawn broke, we got a much clearer idea of the situation. Most of the defensive positions looked like they'd been built by a bunch of kids with poorly stacked sandbags that leaned precariously to one side and odd bits of appropriated wood, building materials and furniture fashioned into bunkers. On the ground were thousands of expended ammunition cases of various calibres and I also found out what type of weapon it was that we had witnessed during our drive between the villages, it was a Mortar Bomb! designed to be used in an indirect fire role, mortars are normally lobbed onto a target, i.e., fired high, in a trajectory that causes the bomb to fall onto the target from above. They had been using it in the direct role, like a rocket.

WHEN THE SMOKE CLEARS

There had been explosions all day as the Artillery bombarded an enemy position in the distance, and we'd all got used to the bangs that echoed around the valley, sending vibrations through our vehicles and bodies as we manoeuvred across the terrain. This bang was different though, louder, and clearer than the rest, it was much closer. I turned around in my seat which was jacked up high, to afford a better firing position, looking back the way we had come, over my left shoulder. To my horror I saw a large black cloud of smoke and dust swirling violently along the line of our convoy. We were a ten-vehicle patrol, and I was at the front. I counted three more Land Rovers between me and the apparent explosion and a couple beyond it.

"All callsigns this is Steve, stand-to, stand-to!" I said into the microphone mounted on my shoulder strap. I didn't know what had happened, but I thought we might be under attack and wanted to be ready to fight. All the vehicles stopped where they were and the blokes manned their weapon systems in a high alert status, scanning the ground around us for signs of the enemy. The dust settled and the smoke cleared, swept away by the light desert wind, to slowly reveal the unmistakeable sight of a Land Rover. Nick, our medic leapt from his seat and began sprinting towards the contorted vehicle as fast as he could with no regard for his own safety, and arrived there quickly, immediately administering first aid to the 3-man crew. The remainder of us held our positions, anticipating a follow-up attack, and the signaller informed HQ of the explosion, which spun-up a medical response team. Once we realised there was no incoming attack, we assumed that it was an IED or a mine, and some more of the blokes close to the damaged vehicle made their way to assist the casualties. Of the three men in the vehicle, Dave L, the driver, miraculously walked away without injury, Dave B the commander suffered life changing injuries, including a broken back, and Damo, the rear gunner was also badly wounded, losing the bottom half of his left leg. Thankfully, there were no fatalities. Eventually it was determined that it was a mine, the first mine strike suffered by the UK of the Operation and probably a legacy anti-tank munition from the Afghan-Soviet War. Fantastic actions by the men on the ground, the medics and recovery forces enabled the safe extraction of all that needed it and the remainder of us returned to base with a renewed respect of the landmine risk as we drove back through the desert. Not long after that incident we received some armour for our Land Rovers. It wasn't very substantial, just some matting, but it might have made a difference to the injuries sustained.

Pathfinder WMIK Land Rover Damaged by Land Mine

-PSYCHOTHERAPY-

IN THE SHADOWS

There was a dark space, maybe it was the inside of an empty warehouse, or it could have been an alleyway behind a block of flats, I couldn't tell. But I could sense the coldness of the air and the sinister quiet. There was no unusual smell just the feeling of the cold air drawing into the nostrils. A man slowly appeared as if illuminated from above by an ice-white light and I could see he had a shaven head that was tilted forward and down. The contrasting temperature between his head and shoulders and the chilly air formed a slight mist above him, and his breath fogged in front of his face as he exhaled. He wore a white sweatshirt but, in the light, it shone a soft grey colour. I recognised that sweatshirt, it was one I owned in the mid-nineties. It was a little bit too big, but I liked the way it made my shoulders look bigger and wore it anyway. It was also the same top I'd been wearing in another vision during a different EMDR session.

"Do you know who the man is?" asked Dr Jackson.

"Yes, it's me." I answered confidently. I was sat in my usual position on the soft chair, feet flat on the carpeted floor, elbows resting on top of my legs mid-thigh, head dropped down facing the ground, eyes closed.

"Stay with that image." She instructed. "Do you get a sense of what you are doing there, in that dark, cold place?"

I focused on the picture in my mind and as my eyes adjusted to the darkness, revealing shadowy figures to my left, shifting forwards and backwards malevolently. Panning around slowly I saw that I was surrounded by featureless men that fidgeted in an agitated way, threatening attack at any moment. It seemed that there was no one directly in front of me, but the space to my left, rear and right was blocked. They wore black clothing that was either a hoodie or a cloak that draped over their heads, casting shadows across their faces. A blurry image, I could only make out dark circles where their eyes and mouth were, almost like the Grim Reaper, they all looked exactly the same, evil. I described this picture in detail to the doctor and tried to convey what the situation felt like. It was like I had gone there to die, like an elephant is said to walk to an elephant cemetery in its final days, but I was hesitant to draw that conclusion.

"I'm there to fight." I said.

My face was also featureless in the image, but it was definitely me I was watching, now standing in a fighting stance with my fists raised beside my head, ready to defend the inevitable attack. It was a strange situation, there was no way I could win the fight, but I had no desire to run, nor to try and negotiate, the fight was going to happen, and the outcome was obvious, I was going to be killed and there was nobody there to help me. The enemy was waiting for one of them to initiate the assault, then they would all join in, swarming on me like ants on a sticky sweet. My heart was beating faster than normal, but not racing, and my breathing was calm and controlled as I waited, poised but not tense.

"How do you feel in that moment, waiting to be attacked?" my psychologist asked.

I considered my answer before saying it out loud because it was unusual, but in that moment, deeply immersed in the scenario, my emotions were clear.

"Happy." I replied. "Happy.......... Excited." I wasn't afraid at all, even though I knew I was about to be killed.

For me, the EMDR sessions were very immersive, dreamlike experiences where it felt real. Sometimes they were memories, sometimes they were fantasy, and sometimes a mixture of both. Sometimes I couldn't distinguish either way. I could tell that I was smiling in the image, almost laughing with excitement. For some reason, I can't remember how that scenario ended but I suppose it suggested that I felt threatened, defensive, lonely, and that death would bring me happiness.

-CHAPTER ELEVEN-

I SEE BAD PEOPLE

HYPERVIGILANCE

When you suffer from hypervigilance you see danger and threats everywhere and never really relax. Every man becomes a potential adversary and every situation a potential disaster or battle ground. Without realising it was abnormal, I spent several years of my life thinking like that, in a perpetual state of high readiness, anticipating violence or incident constantly. As a paratrooper this mindset can be a great asset, especially on tours of duty, because you are rarely caught off guard or surprised and you are always planning your reaction to unplanned events. However, as a civilian walking down the High Street it's not so good, and psychologically preparing for a fight, dozens of times during a quick trip to the shops takes its toll. Physical preparation also takes place with small subconscious actions like taking hands out of pockets to enable faster punching, clenching the jaw, and tucking the chin to reduce the impact from incoming strikes. To a lot of soldiers this would seem perfectly normal behaviour, and it was to me too, until a psychologist explained otherwise. These types of physical adjustments can be noticed by approaching strangers who in response might begin to perform similar actions themselves, creating a self-fulfilling prophecy. I used to think that people were always acting aggressively towards me, but my psychologist suggested I might be eliciting a reaction from them through my own aggressive posture.

For those who do not have a hypervigilant personality it's probably hard to imagine, but I can try to explain it with a scenario that I have experienced many times:
Walking to town with my wife and 2 children I often cross a

narrow footbridge over a river. When I see other men walking towards me on that bridge my mind races through several thoughts:

Who are they with?

Do they look aggressive or suspicious?

Are they drunk or drugged?

What will I do if they bump into one of my family or say something offensive?

Do they look like they can handle themselves?

Have they got weapons?

Can I overpower them?

Who should I attack first?

Will they hurt my family?

Will my family put themselves in danger trying to protect me?

How will my family cope if they see me hurt or killed?

How will they cope if they witness me killing someone?

Am I prepared to fight to the death if the situation escalates?

If I go to prison can we afford our house?

Where would my family live if we have to sell the house?

How will they cope psychologically if I go to prison for murder?

Medication and psychotherapy have taken the edge off it for me and although I seldom experience happiness or enjoyment, I am able to switch off a lot more than I could before. Trying not to look at people, avoiding crowded places and understanding my triggers also reduce the anxiety and stress.

When I joined the army, as recruits we were constantly reminded of the IRA threat and our training was often delivered around a terrorist scenario. Our instructors taught us to always be vigilant and look out for the "presence of the abnormal or absence of the normal." When put on Guard Duty we would patrol around camp in pairs checking everything for signs of tampering or IED's, bins, lamp posts, drains, manhole covers, doors, windows. Recruits from other Regiments would walk around the perimeter in 5 minutes, but we'd take an hour. I remember the first time we had weekend leave and one of the Corporals gave us some advice before we left for the train station.

"If someone pulls up in a car and starts shooting at you, do not fucking run away!" He said intensely. "Run at them! Run at them as fast as you can, and fucking kill them with whatever you've got! They will shit their pants if you do that, they won't expect it, they'll expect you to run away, but paratroopers don't run away from fucking anybody!"

I loved that shit! Our Corporals were awesome, and I knew that they would react just like they wanted us to. They were all Northern Ireland veterans and were wired tight.

THE BEST DEFENCE IS
A VIOLENT OFFENSE

One day I was driving through my hometown after visiting a friend who owns an army surplus store there. Leaving his shop, I made my way towards a roundabout to complete a U-turn. On my left, a car appeared from a minor road and waited for me to go past before pulling out behind me. As soon as I saw the vehicle, I was suspicious, there were two men in it that I had never seen before, both with unkempt beards. They drove close behind me, and I watched them follow in my interior mirror, as I got to the roundabout and turned back the way I had come towards my friends shop. This was suspicious because they could have easily turned right at the junction and avoided the roundabout. My heartrate started to increase and my grip on the steering wheel tightened when they turned left at the next junction right behind me and crossed over the road bridge which spans the river. I was rocking in my seat now and getting angry. "You fuckers think you are going to get me? Fuck you! I'm gonna get you!" I was saying to myself. The car followed me at the next junction too, and at that point I decided I was not going to go home and lead them to my house so they could hurt my family, or butcher me in front of them. I knew a place nearby where the road narrowed just wide enough for a car to get through. I would drive through it, then stop. The car behind would then be stuck in the narrow space, unable to open their doors to get out and I would launch my attack, running to the driver's side, where the window was down, and start punching him in the head as hard and fast as I could, screaming at the passenger the whole time that he was next. The next junction approached, and I indicated left, watching in the mirror to see what they would do. Sure enough they also indicated left. I was extremely wound up now, the adrenaline was surging through me and I felt strong and focussed, I was excited. At the junction I went straight on. If they followed, after already indicating left, then I was going to initiate my trap at the next junction about 300 metres down the road. They turned left and disappeared out of sight, never to be seen again. I told Dr Jackson about that situation on my next session, and she asked me what I thought would have happened if they had followed me.

"I would have executed my plan." I answered. "I was on my way there, it would have happened."

"What would have been the result if they were innocent guys who just happened to be going that way?" she asked.

"I'd be in prison." I said sadly.

Good psychologists don't have to say a lot. She knew what that meant to me, abandoning my family was the worst outcome possible and that really got me thinking.

BAD COP, WORSE COP

In 2006 we were not only the first British army unit in Afghanistan to take casualties from a mine-strike, but we were also the first to get into a contact. The night it happened we were patrolling to a town that had not been visited before and had no real intelligence about. I had planned the route and led the way as the front vehicle, driving through the night and lying-up during the day to remain discrete. Our intention was to get into a position of overwatch on the town during darkness, observe the activity at the start of the day, then call the police chief on the phone and arrange a meeting. We got within a few hundred metres of our intended halt position when a burst of automatic gunfire went straight over the top of us, the red tracer rounds visible as they zipped past. We stopped and I traversed my GPMG to the right, towards where the shots had come from. I didn't return fire immediately because I couldn't identify the firing point, I just had a rough idea because of the tracer trajectory. The next burst they fired gave me a much better idea where they were and I shot back, along with my rear gunner and a load of the guys in the vehicles behind me, our bullets converging on the hill ahead in a hail of 7.62mm and .50cal tracer. They fired back with equal intensity though and we executed a contact drill, to extract ourselves from the open ground we were in, turning the vehicles around one at a time and heading back the way we'd come from to our emergency rendezvous point (ERV). During the manoeuvre one of our vehicles lost traction on the edge of a wadi and rolled onto its roof, luckily not crushing anyone in the process. The incoming fire was pretty accurate, and we could hear it snapping past and banging on the metal of the vehicles, so we decided to abandon the recovery of the downed wagon and get the blokes out of the killing zone. Before moving off again I tried to confirm that the three blokes from that vehicle were safely on board another, but only got confirmation on two. Worried that one might be trapped or injured I quickly jumped off and ran back to the vehicle behind me. "Is Chuck on your wagon?" I shouted.

They had one of the others, but not Chuck, so I ran to the next vehicle and shouted the same question. This time I heard Chuck's unmistakeable Midland's voice as he shouted back.

"I'm on here Steve, I'm all good mate." He said clearly and calmly.

"Nice one, cheers mate. Let's go!" I yelled.

We got everyone out of there safely and regrouped in some cover on a reverse slope about one kilometre away, positioning some of the vehicles so the rear gunners could still observe the enemy position and engage with their long-range weapons if needed. The Afghans also had long range weapons and continued to fire at us sporadically. Even though they couldn't see us, because of their knowledge of the terrain, they knew where we were. One of our Forward Air Controllers was already co-ordinating an airstrike onto the enemy position when I was told that eight men were firing and manoeuvring towards our stricken vehicle. There was no way an airstrike would arrive in time to stop them pillaging our wagon, so we decided to deny it ourselves with an anti-tank missile. I walked over to the vehicle with the Milan anti-tank missile system mounted on the roof to speak to the firer and as I did, I could hear the rounds hitting the rocks and stones on the ground around me, right at the limit of their range. The soldier, observing through the thermal imaging sight gave me a live update of what he could see and as they neared the vehicle, we fired the missile, which sent them running and deterred them from trying again. The airstrike seemed to be taking a long time to materialise, so I pursued it over the radio and was told there was some ongoing dialogue at a higher level causing a delay.

By the time we got any news it was daylight and it had been concluded that we were fighting with the Afghan Police, who had mistaken us for Taliban fighters. Our boss was given the phone number of the police chief and after a brief conversation it became apparent that we indeed were. Everyone was told to stop firing and not engage, and we cautiously moved to an agreed meeting point, which was our abandoned wagon. The Afghanis raced there as fast as they could in their Toyota Hilux's, beating us to it and immediately clambering over the wreckage to steal whatever they could get their hands on. Our blokes weren't far behind and quickly apprehended the police who tried to disappear with their kit and secured the area. The police were a ramshackle mob, a few wore a blue uniform, but most wore traditional civilian clothing, making it impossible to differentiate them from the public. As soon as I started talking to one of them, he started asking for stuff. Water, food, batteries, medical supplies and best of all – ammunition! Through the interpreter he complained about the lack of ammunition they had remaining after they'd expended most of their stock on us.

"Tell him I'll see what I can do." I said insincerely, there was absolutely no way in hell I was going to resupply them with ammo, after they'd only just stopped trying to kill us.

To gain some information on their defensive position I went up the hill with a couple of vehicles to have a look and take some notes and sketches.

At the top of the hill was a trench system and underground bunker, all fortified with large sandbags, many of which had U.N symbols printed on them from their original use as bags of grain or rice. Our ammunition had done a fair amount of damage to their defences and a few of the police were walking around with bloodied bandages too. One had wounds to his hand, another to his head and apparently some had been extracted into the town by motorbike for medical treatment. My mate Leon kept watch for me with his GPMG from the turret of the vehicle and I noticed two of the police staring at him and whispering to each other excitedly.

"What are they talking about?" I asked the interpreter suspiciously.

He conversed with them and they giggled effeminately. "They like Leon." He said. "They say he looks like a little boy."

One of the men made a gesture, making a circle with the forefinger and thumb of one hand and poking the forefinger of the other hand through it a few times.

"What did he fucking say?" called Leon. "Are they talking about me?"

"Tell them fuckers that he is not a boy, and he will fucking kill them if they carry on like that!" I ordered the interpreter, before answering Leon. "Ignore them mate, they're taking the piss." I said.

Looking around the position I used the interpreter to find out about the situation and learned that there were about twelve policemen that worked there, who hadn't been paid and couldn't go home because it was too dangerous. There were also two fourteen-year-old boys who worked there, who's exact role was hard to determine despite my persistence to ascertain. Eventually he told me and spoke like it was obvious, and I was stupid to ask.

"They are for fucking!" he said with a shrug of the shoulders.

I felt sick but showed no emotion. "Okay, and what else do these boys do here?" I asked.

Realising my ignorance, he laid it out nice and clear for me. "They are not for cooking, they are not for cleaning, they are for fucking!" he explained, without batting an eyelid.

The police were also looking at me as he translated for them, clearly not in the least bit concerned about me knowing.

"And out of the twelve policemen that work here, how many are having sex with these boys?" I asked, suppressing my desire to kill them right there and then.

He answered me without even conversing with the others and spoke like I was asking a silly question. "All of them of course!"

he replied.

While I was up there a Chinook helicopter had flown in to re-cover our Land Rover and resupply us with ammunition. To my amazement they also brought ammunition for the Afghans too, at the request of my boss. They were bad men, and I wasn't even convinced they were police. I think they knew exactly who they were shooting at and I think they were raping young boys in that bunker. Later on, I questioned the ethics of their actions to the interpreter and his defensive response was. "They cannot see their wives because they are on that hill, what do you expect them to do?"

"I fucking expect them to not rape children!" I replied.

Four of the police and a PF soldier

The wrecked Land Rover WMIK

I'D RATHER BE SHOT THAN MAULED

In Macedonia we'd get dispatched to lots of different villages or scenes to conduct liaison tasks or gather information, sometimes at short notice, sometimes pre planned. Many times, I would just be following the vehicle in front with little idea of what was going on. One day we were sent to a village that we had been to a few times before in the Tetovo Valley and that's exactly what I was doing, following the wagon in front, confident that the patrol commander would update me when appropriate. It was a rural place controlled by the Macedonian Army, with a small number of soldiers and armoured vehicles defending it. The soldiers and the local population did not like us and deeply resented us being there. The first time we visited I was talking to some men in the Village Square in an attempt to build some rapport, but it was obvious they did not want to converse by their short answers and failure to look at me when talking. I noticed an accent in one of them who spoke good English.

"You sound Australian." I said.

"I was born there." He replied.

That was an opportunity to get some dialogue going and I did my best to exploit it, talking to him about his early childhood in Australia and how he'd come to be a Macedonian citizen. After that I thought I had an ally in the village.

In depot, my Section Commander, Cpl Fletcher used to tell us stories about his tours in Northern Ireland and one of the things he said to look out for on patrol was "Absence of the normal or presence of the abnormal."

Entering the village outskirts that day, I was in the rear veh4icle and we followed the others along the quiet country lane. There was no traffic and unusually nobody outside, normally there would be children playing in the street or front gardens of the big farmhouses. I also noticed a few tractors were parked on driveways and caught a glimpse of some adults peering at us from behind a back garden wall as we passed. I would later kick myself for not reacting to these absences of the normal and presences of the abnormal. When we arrived at the Village Square, I noticed the ex-Aussie sitting in his usual spot and acknowledged him with a wave, which he returned. After a couple of minutes, the patrol commander, led by a Macedonian soldier and followed by the other vehicles in our patrol left the square to investigate something. I was told to stay put, which left me and the driver on our own in the Square. Within seconds the Square began to fill up with people and I heard the voice of my patrol commander on the radio, asking me where I was.

"Confirm locstat." he said.

"Roger, we are still in the Square." I replied. Thinking it was pretty obvious.

He came back on the radio and calmly updated me on a rapidly changing situation. "Be aware, that we are now outside of the village and unable to get back to you as the roads have been blocked by tractors and cars."

My mate was also wearing an earpiece so we both knew we were cut off from the others as the locals started to approach our vehicle menacingly. All of a sudden, we were completely surrounded by screaming men and women who were banging on the windows and bodywork of the wagon angrily, rocking it side to side. I placed my rifle horizontally across my lap and released the safety catch.

"Drive!" I said firmly. The muzzle was touching the metal door, pointing at the body of a crazed woman whose face was pressed against the window, spitting on it as she screamed hysterically. I looked at my mate in the driver's seat. "If that door opens, I'm gonna start fucking shooting!" I warned him.

He was from a different regiment than me and did not share my aggressive, airborne mentality.

"Calm down mate." He offered. "We'll be alright." He revved the engine and attempted to move forward but they did not move.

"Fucking run them over if you need to mate, we need to go!" I was calm but conscious of the danger we were in. I was thinking of the brutal murders of Corporals Wood and Howes in Northern Ireland, who had been dragged from their vehicle by a baying mob and killed in 1988. The video footage of that terrible incident was ingrained in my memory.

"I am not getting dragged out of this fucking wagon mate!" I told him.

I'd already noticed a Macedonian soldier who stood close by on a bit of high ground watching the melee. We had exchanged glances briefly and he had given me a sinister grin, and thought that if I started firing, he would probably shoot me. That was a better option. I'd much rather get shot than torn apart by these bastards. Slowly we crept forwards and the lunatics were sensible enough to step aside enabling us to get out of the Square and re-unite with the others who had cleared the roadblock. I'll never know what their intention was that day, but I do know that I wasn't getting dragged out of that vehicle without killing some fuckers first.

YOU CAN'T CHOOSE
YOUR FAMILY

I never knew any of my grandparents and they all died long ago. My mum detested her father and disliked her mother. My dad's father died when he was young, and his mother wanted nothing to do with my brother and I for some reason. At a very young age, I did meet both of my grandmothers once each though. I saw my mum's mum in a hospice just before she died, and we gave her a bedside visit to say hello and goodbye. I can't remember what her face looked like, but I remember she was old, grey, frail, and lying on a bed with light blue sheets, and the floor was painted red. I think she gave us a box of Maltesers chocolates to take with us when we left. After that we went to her house to check on her dog, but I never saw it, just heard it barking from the kitchen. We didn't stay long because my mum hated being in that house, it brought back too many unhappy memories from her childhood.

My dad took us to see his mum once too, I don't know why, she wasn't even dying yet! She wasn't interested, but we were excited to be there, because we also got to meet two uncles we knew nothing about too. David was my dad's younger brother, but he didn't really talk and just went to his bedroom upstairs. Ashley was my dad's adopted or half-brother, who was the youngest of them all at about fourteen years old, and the only one who engaged with me and my brother. While the adults talked, Ashley invited us to play outside and we followed him out the front door and through a dark, enclosed alleyway that ran between the terraced houses to the rear garden. Shortly afterwards we walked back into the alleyway with me leading the way. I had almost reached the end of the tunnel when Ashley spoke.

"Turn around!" he called out.

I turned to see him stood behind my brother with his left arm draped high across his chest, holding him in place. In his other hand was a long screwdriver that he held to the side of his neck, the tip making an indentation as he pressed it against the skin.

"I'm going to fucking kill your brother!" he said.

"Let him go!" I shouted angrily.

"If you don't do what I say, I'll stick this right through his neck, and he'll die!" Ashley snapped.

My brother looked terrified but managed to tell me. "Get dad, now!"

I sprinted into the house and got my dad, and when we came back out Ashley had gone, leaving my brother behind, shaken up, but unharmed. My only other memory of that visit is the sound of Ashley receiving the belt from his dad upstairs. We could hear the leather whipping his body as he screamed in pain and pleaded for mercy. Play silly games, get silly prizes! We never saw any of them again after that.

-PSYCHOTHERAPY-

GO DRIVE OFF A BRIDGE

Where I live there is a viaduct that I usually drive across twice every day going to and from work. It stands about one hundred and fifty feet above the river and its adjacent fields, spans a length of about ¼ of a mile and is approached on both sides by steep-sided slopes which means you easily hit it at 60mph. A while ago I realised that I could gauge my state of mind by how I feel on that road, because I think about smashing through the barriers and driving off the edge a lot, sometimes every single day, for months at a time. I imagine slamming through the waist-high concrete wall and falling to my death. Sometimes the car flips over the wall and somersaults violently until impact and sometimes it blasts straight through like a rocket but plummets quite peacefully. Either way I just sit there calmly, almost in a trance. I imagine how the car would look and sound depending on what surface it landed on. It could be high tide where it dives underwater, strikes the riverbed, and resurfaces, momentarily floating with the tide for a few seconds until all of the air is expelled and it sinks again, or low tide where it thuds into the riverbed, embedding itself a couple of feet into the thick mud and sticking out like a crumpled wreck. I've never linked it to my own experience until this very moment as I write about it, but years ago, my brother was talking to me when he said. "You know when you're driving along, and

209

you start thinking about killing yourself?"

I didn't know how to respond to that back then, because I had never had such thoughts. "What do you mean?" I asked.

"You know." He explained. "When you look at a bridge or a wall and think how easy it would be to kill yourself by driving off it, or into it!"

"Not really mate, no." I replied. I couldn't relate to it then, but I can now, and I can also see how he thought it was normal behaviour as well, because he'd probably felt like that for so long, he'd forgotten what normal behaviour was.

Trees are another structure that get your attention when you have suicidal thoughts. Many times, I've stopped still in the forest while out walking with my dog to study a tree. As a survival and bushcraft enthusiast I've taken time to learn about different tree species and I appreciate their utility for shelter building, yielding edible fruits and nuts, and fire lighting. As someone who often has suicidal thoughts, I sometimes look at trees and assess them for other properties such as suitably strong enough branches to hold my weight, accessibility to get a rope into the right position, concealment from passing dog walkers and joggers, and how easy their location would be to describe in a suicide message so I could be recovered by the right people. As a practitioner of martial arts, especially grappling and Brazilian Jiu Jitsu, I have learned what it feels like to get choked out, and from my own experiences, the thought of being strangled to death does not perturb me at all, because I know that the feeling before going unconscious is actually quite euphoric. I've also imagined a mixture of both suicide options many times and considered jumping off the viaduct with a rope around my neck, wondering if the rope would choke me, break my neck, or decapitate me, depending on the rope length and thickness. Doing that would also run a high risk of local people, including children, being exposed to the graphic image of my dead body hanging from the bridge or lying on the ground below, and that is not something I would want to put on them.

-CHAPTER TWELVE-

DOCTOR'S ORDERS

DR. DO-VERY-LITTLE

An army doctor cut a small lump of flesh from my thigh once after I went to see him complaining that it was hurting. I've still got the scar to prove it. The previous day I'd been play fighting with a friend and thrown him into some bushes. As he'd fallen down backwards, he'd grabbed hold of me and I'd stepped into the bush with him, getting a large thorn or part of a stick stuck in my leg as I did so. I didn't notice it straight away, but a few minutes later it started to hurt, and I dropped my trousers to have a look. It looked like a foreign object was in my leg, so I went to get some tweezers from my locker to extract it. When I sat back down, I could no longer see the object, but when I tensed my leg, a lump protruded a surprising length out from the site. I assumed that whatever was in there had either buried in deeper, or come out, but I couldn't find anything inside my clothes or on the floor. The next morning, when I stepped out of bed, it was really painful and the lump was still there, so I went to the Medical Centre to get it checked out. The doctor was an army Captain and after he'd heard what happened and had a quick look, he declared he was going to perform a mini operation to retrieve the object. He sat me down in the treatment room and called out to one of the Para Reg medics who also worked there.

"Vince, come and watch this. I'm doing a mini op." he shouted.

Vince was a mate of mine, a big strong bloke who did a lot of weight training. He enjoyed medical stuff, so he'd got posted to the Med Centre for a while to further his knowledge and skills. He came in and sat down. The Doc wiped my leg with some wipes then injected some local anaesthetic into the area of the lump. A couple of minutes later he made his first incision and cut down next to the small hole, trying to expose the thorn, but didn't find it. After a couple of minutes fiddling around he'd cut out a small piece of flesh, but not found anything, and said he'd have to stop because the local anaesthetic wouldn't suffice if he went any deeper. "I think you'll feel it if I go any further." He advised.

"I can already feel it now Doc." I admitted.

"We better stop here and get you sewn up then." He said, before giving me a couple of internal, and a few external stitches.

He hadn't found a thorn or discovered what was causing the protrusion so explained to me that he was going to send the piece of flesh away to be investigated. Even if they didn't find a thorn, they could still at least rule out anything more sinister. He turned around to the table then turned back, obviously looking for something. "Vince, did you see where I put that lump?" he asked.

Vince answered awkwardly "Last time I saw it, it was on the scalpel handle boss."

The Doc thought hard for a second "Damn it, I've thrown it in the sharps bin with the scalpel." He said before turning back to me. "It was probably nothing anyway. Come back in a week to get the stitches out. No running and no weight training on that leg."

There was no way anyone was going into the sharps bin with all the blades and needles that were in there. I bet none of that is on my medical records though!

In my old Platoon we had a rule where if someone managed to stand directly behind you and place their hands on your shoulders you had to give them a "piggy-back." There was no arguing, it didn't matter where you were, or what you were wearing, that was the law. There were also some recognised commands that had to be obeyed; "Bunk me up!" meant you had to shuck them up higher on your back, even if they were already as high as possible. If they kicked their feet in front of you it meant you had to run, and you couldn't stop running until they held their feet out together in front of you with their toes curled back, and you had to go wherever they said. All commands were delivered with a deliberately nasty, humiliating tone and the only one that you wanted to hear was "Put me down!" Our camp in Dover was at the top of a very big, steep hill and sometimes you would get caught at the bottom of it and get absolutely beasted, but it could happen anywhere, in a shopping centre, a pub, or on camp. The only thing that restrained the blokes was the knowledge that at some point, revenge would be taken, and that knowledge worked like a nuclear deterrent for most. One Sunday night we had just left a bar called "J's" when my mate Scotty, a big bloke weighing about fifteen stones jumped on my back without warning, not even putting his hands on my shoulders first, he just ran and jumped on me. In my drunken state I instinctively grabbed hold of his legs to catch him, but not being braced, I toppled forwards and slammed my head into the paving-slabbed ground, absorbing the full force with my forehead because I didn't think to put my hands out. Standing up dazed, everyone was laughing until they saw the cuts to my head and stopped for a few seconds. Scotty apologised and I gave him a bit of grief for breaking the rules before we carried on to the next pub, the "Ellie" just around the corner. One of the girls who worked behind the bar was quite concerned about my injuries and suggested I went to hospital, but I told her I was alright, and she kindly cleaned me up as best she could with tissue and water in the ladies toilet. As the night went on my head began to swell, but the pubs closed early because of Sunday opening hours and we went back to camp at about 2230hrs and I got my head down for the night. In the morning, the swelling on my forehead was quite significant and accompanied by a headache, so I went to the Med Centre to get checked out. Now sober, I realised I could have done some real damage, but the Army doctor dismissed my concerns and predictably sent me away with a bit of Ibuprofen and some sage advice along the lines of "Avoid headbutting concrete for the next two weeks." The next day the swelling had got even worse and almost closed my eyes and when my friend Matt saw me, he advised me to go to the local hospital for a second opinion. I told him what the Doc had said and that I'd be alright, but he insisted and took me in his own car to Dover Hospital, where they called in a neurologist. His opinion was that the wounds to my forehead were infected and the swelling was working its way down my face because of gravity, which was likely to spread the infection to my eyes unless treated immediately. He gave me a thorough check-over, x-rayed my skull, cleaned, and dressed the cuts, then prescribed antibiotics and told me to lie flat on my back as much as possible to reduce the swelling on my face. The next time I saw the Army doctor he made a point of bringing up my disloyalty. The hospital had sent him the paperwork for my visit and after he gave me his diagnosis at the end of the consultation, he made a point by saying, "But if you don't trust my opinion, you can always go to the hospital in town and ask them."

"Maybe I will Sir." I said.

He was a shit doctor!

TINNITUS

Tinnitus is the name of the condition where someone experiences "ringing in their ears." Its onset can be for several reasons, but in the Army, it is often because of exposure to loud noise. For several years I said to medics and doctors that I found hearing tests difficult because I could always hear a high pitch beeping / whistling in my ears when sat in the silence of the testing booth with headphones on. Other blokes would often say the same when we were talking about the test, and we didn't know it, but we had tinnitus. I don't know why the medics or doctors failed to pursue it, maybe they assumed we knew, or maybe they just wanted to get the test done and get on with the next patient. I had it explained to me by an audiology doctor in Plymouth after being referred to him when my test results showed a deterioration. I remember saying to him. "I don't know if it's normal, but I find the high pitch beeps on the test really hard to hear because I can't tell if it's the noise in my ears, or the noise of the headphones."

Surprisingly, there was no record of it in my documents, but he explained about tinnitus to me, and it made sense. Not long after that, after an MRI scan and a few appointments with different specialists I was fitted with a hearing aid and issued a tinnitus pillow, which turned out to be a pillow with a small speaker inside that you can play other sounds on to mask the ringing. Great idea, and the sound of falling rain or birds singing did distract me for sure, however it kept my wife awake, so I stopped using it. Some people become depressed from the constant noise in their head or ears, and it has even led to cases of suicide. There is no escaping it, it's always there and certain things can make it worse. For me, stress, tiredness, and low mood exacerbate it. Every now and then I realise that I can't hear it, but as soon as I have that thought, it comes on extra loud. Another time it's extra loud is when someone asks about it. You can go for hours without being conscious of it because you are distracted or focused on something else, but as soon as someone mentions it, the ringing comes back to the forefront. I've even brought it on myself and others before when I've stupidly asked them.

"How is your tinnitus?" Nobody with the condition will ever thank you for asking that!

Regardless of how it was before the question, it inevitably gets worse immediately afterwards, and not only does it set theirs off, but it also sets mine off too. A while ago someone was telling me how they needed complete silence to sleep, and as I tried to imagine it, I realised that I would never experience silence again. I can't imagine how severely the men from World War One and Two must have suffered with hearing damage, imagine being on an artillery gun position, with no hearing defence and constantly firing barrages of shells. Hearing damage is permanent, and the military do issue service people with protective equipment, but unfortunately you don't normally get a chance to don them when someone starts shooting at you. Instead of removing your helmet to put them on, your priority and that of everyone around you, is to return fire and concentrate on not getting killed. I remember one day I had it really bad, and I was looking forward to getting to the beach, where we were running some survival training. The sea was rough, and I thought the sound of the crashing waves would mask it, but it didn't, and that very loud period lasted for several weeks.

On the advice of doctors, I submitted a compensation claim for my hearing loss. They advised me that the frequency range where I have deafness is caused by exposure to explosions and loud bangs such as gunfire. They all also agreed that my hearing loss and tinnitus were caused by my service, nobody disputes that. My claim was rejected on the grounds that it was submitted too late. There was a set period of time from point of injury or point of diagnosis when you had to initiate a claim, but like most soldiers, I did not knowingly injure my ears. I considered my point of diagnosis as the point I was told I needed a hearing aid. Even though it is acknowledged that I've been deafened and suffered tinnitus through service activities and events, someone trawled through my medical records to find an anomaly and exploit it to reject my claim.

SEEKING HELP

The first time I asked for psychological support was very difficult, and I completely empathise with people who are reluctant
to do it. Getting the words out is hard, but it's also an instant
relief, and when I finally verbalised it, I broke down in tears.
The doctor I saw was a civilian who worked in a military Medical Centre, and she quickly arranged for me to visit a Mental
Health Practice. That first visit was a disaster that I'm certain
worsened and prolonged my mental health issues. First of all,
the nurse I met was a young Royal Navy, Junior Non-commissioned Officer, wearing uniform who acted very formally, and
asked very difficult questions. As a Parachute Regiment Colour
Sergeant, it was unusual for me to be talking to a servicewoman,
and even more unusual for me to be talking to a junior rank
about my personal problems. I thought it would have been so
much easier if she'd been wearing civilian clothes and dispensed
with the formalities of rank and service. After the standard
questions and answers I was taken to a desk in a different office
with a computer on it and asked to complete a digital questionnaire. The nurse sat in an adjacent desk, behind another computer and I wondered if she was monitoring my on-screen answers as I went through them. On completion of the test, I was
taken back to the consultation room and told to wait while the
results were analysed. Returning with some sheets of paper the
nurse returned to give me her assessment.
"We've looked at your results." she said. "And according to how
you've answered, we don't think you have PTSD."
I was taken aback; nobody had even suggested that, least of all
me. "I never said I did have PTSD!" I replied defensively. I didn't
want that label.

She went on to basically tell me that I was ok and could go home and I walked out of there wondering what the hell had just happened and feeling like I'd been wasting peoples time.

About four years later in 2014 I was in a post that I hated in Army HQ and coming to the end of my military career, still struggling psychologically. For about eight years I had experienced very little happiness or enjoyment and a lot of anger and depression. The catalyst that made me seek help one more time was when I smashed my vacuum cleaner into the floor in front of my children and saw the frightened look on their faces. I was already in a bad mood about something, and my wife had walked past and made a comment that pushed me over the edge. For a second I was so enraged, I wanted to kill her, but I was just about in control enough not to. Instead, I picked up the vacuum cleaner up, high above my head. Within a nano second, I'd resisted the urge to throw it through the front window and the television and decided to slam it into the stone tiled living room floor. My wife then antagonised me further.
"That's clever, now the Hoover's broken!" she said sarcastically. My anger had already spiked, so I was past the point of potential violence, but still very angry.
"It was either that or smash it over your head!" I snapped.
It was then I realised my kids were watching, and they looked scared. That hit me hard, even in that moment of rage. I was acting like my mother's ex-boyfriend who terrified me and gave me nightmares, because of his violence towards her. Recollecting that incident now, still fills me with shame and regret and I think it probably had a psychologically damaging effect on my children, who were around six and eight years old at the time. Writing it down, I'm considering deleting it because it will shape opinions on me, we'll see.
This time when I went to the Medical Centre, I saw a military doctor and it was another awkward conversation. Not because of him, he was on-the-ball, but because it's a very hard subject to broach. The doctor was probably expecting to hear about a

twisted ankle or a chest infection, but instead I told him that I really needed help, because I thought I was a bit mental, that I was likely to kill somebody that didn't deserve to be killed, and that I didn't want to leave the army as a "basket case." Like my previous appeal, this acknowledgement and plea for help opened the floodgates and I started to sob pathetically. I say pathetically, not in a derogatory way, but in a sad way, because it is sad to see a grown man, especially a soldier, so vulnerable and broken, it makes me feel sad just to picture it. The doctor gave me a moment to collect myself, which I did quickly before wiping my eyes and sitting up straight, like I'd turned my emotions off with the flick of a switch. I explained my circumstances to him, and he offered to put me on some drugs immediately, which I accepted, hoping they would work like a magic pill. I began taking anti-depression medication and was placed on the waiting list to see a mental health specialist nurse as an urgent case. I remember the instant that I realised the drugs were working. It wasn't because I felt happy or de-stressed, it was when I noticed that I was watching my kids run down the road without worrying. Normally, I'd be highly stressed, thinking about them falling over and what type of injuries they'd sustain if they hit a wall, lamp post or the ground and I'd be looking out for cars, or people getting into cars, and open gates or doors where a dog could run out from, and spillages or slippery surfaces. All these scenarios would race through my mind, and I'd run through my options of dealing with them in the event they happened. This time was different though, for the first time ever, I wasn't stressing, they were just running down a hill and would probably be alright.

It wasn't long until I saw the mental health nurse who was very professional this time and after a few sessions she referred me to the Psychologist. One day, after an hour-long session where I felt like I was making progress, I walked out of the Medical centre towards my workplace and passed a man in a suit who was walking in the opposite direction. I'd looked up at him to acknowledge him, but he was looking the other way, so I kept quiet and walked on, but as soon as we passed each other I thought I heard him mutter "Fucking Squaddies!" and my mind started racing. Trying to rationalise why I might have angered him, I guessed that maybe he had also looked up to acknowledge me and thought I'd ignored him. I closed my eyes and took a couple of deep breaths as I walked. "Leave it! It doesn't matter!" I said out loud to myself. Just hearing the word "Squaddie" is enough to anger a paratrooper, as it is a repulsive word that we do not use or acknowledge as representative of us. I turned around and ran after him, ironically heading back towards the Med Centre where I'd just been learning how to manage my anger.

"Oi!" I shouted loudly.

The man stopped and turned to face me, as I jogged up to him.

"What did you just fucking say to me?" I asked aggressively.

He looked confused. "Eh? I didn't say anything mate." He replied.

"Yes, you fucking did! You said, "Fucking Squaddies" or something like that as you went past." I told him.

"No, I didn't. Why would I say that?" he stated, shaking his head.

I persisted. "Did you say hello, and think I fucking ignored you or something?"

He paused for thought, then explained that he'd said, "For fuck's sake!" when he'd noticed some vehicles in the car park.

"See those white vans?" he said. "Yesterday, I told my contractors not to park them there, and twats have done it again, because they're too lazy to walk an extra thirty seconds to the office." He pointed to four white vans parked side-by-side in the Med Centre car park. "Anyway, I'm an ex-squaddie." He said, pointing to my Sergeant Major rank badge. "I left as a Sergeant Major myself two years ago."

I believed him, he seemed like a genuine bloke and after a short chat we went our separate ways without incident.

The psychologist who I saw during that period, Dr Beuster was really good, and I think he genuinely cared about helping me. He even phoned me on my mobile phone to check in with me a couple of times. Talking to him helped me understand what was going on in my head a lot more and gave me some coping mechanisms to deal with my hypervigilance, anger, and anxiety. Along with the medication, those first few sessions settled me down quite a bit and I had far fewer urges to attack people that I thought might be out to get me.

MY THERAPIST DRIVES ME MAD

"I'm alright now, but I've got to be honest with you, if you'd said the wrong thing a minute ago, I was going to jump over that desk and start punching your fucking head in!" I said calmly.

"Oh, okay, well there's no need for that, I'm not here to upset you." Ralph said, rather taken aback.

"I know that now, but I'd already made my mind up and it would have happened." I kindly clarified. "But I'm alright now, I'm not thinking that anymore, I've calmed down."

This is something I once said to a psychotherapist during a consultation. It was the last time I had therapy with him, I got assigned to someone else, this time a Clinical Psychologist. Ralph was actually a great bloke and after we parted ways as client and therapist, we got on well as friends, but that day he really pushed my buttons and I was very close to attacking him in his office, barely keeping control of myself. I'd had a few sessions with Ralph after being transferred from the Mental Health clinic in Tidworth to the one in Plymouth. It was frustrating, because I'd already gone through the whole assessment and evaluation process at Tidworth, starting with a referral from the G.P, seeing a Mental Health Nurse for a few weeks, then a Psychiatrist and then regular appointments with a Clinical Psychologist. I was quite angry because the sessions at Tidworth had helped me a lot and I felt like I was progressing, but moving locations seemed to put me back to the bottom of the list, and here I was, answering the same questions I'd been asked long before, giving the same answers. It made me think nobody was listening, or they couldn't be bothered to read my notes, because most of it was historical and not subject to change anyway and I'd already been diagnosed with PTSD.

Before the session I'd been sat in the waiting area filling out the usual questionnaire which asks questions like:
"In the last 2 weeks how often have you had thoughts of self-harm or suicide?"
"In the last 2 weeks how often have you experienced little or no enjoyment in doing things?"
There are multiple answers but mine would often be "Every day" and when I'd sit down and get asked how I was feeling after handing that questionnaire over, I'd wonder what the point was. To be honest it wasn't just the questionnaire that wound me up in that waiting area, the whole layout frustrated me. There were signs everywhere, in no discernible order, in different colours, sizes, fonts and orientation. Some signs such as the "If you have been waiting for longer than ten minutes please speak to a member of Reception Staff," were duplicated in several locations on the same wall with slight variations in the detail. Some notices were dated from several years before and signed by people who had undoubtedly moved on to another job. There were even two different comments and suggestions boxes. It looked like a bunch of busy bodies had been let loose in there without consulting each other and just filled the walls with stereo typical bullshit. If you were there to treat OCD, you were in a world of pain! Nobody talked in there either, a senior Naval Officer could be sat next to a Royal Marine who peeked at his clipboard while he ticked boxes about wishing he were dead or had been sniffing glue while dressed as a German pig farmer. It was awkward because whoever walked in, you assumed they were fucked up, and you knew they were thinking the same about you. You were probably both right!

In that session I said something about depression to Ralph and then said something like; "Depression is one of the symptoms of my PTSD right?" I wasn't really asking a question, just getting to my point, but his response was a question.

"Is it?" He said.

I was immediately irritated. "What do you mean?" I quizzed.

"Well, is it one of your symptoms?" He responded.

"Well, I think so. You tell me, you're the therapist." I wasn't sure if he was leading me down a path of enlightenment or deliberately trying to antagonise me, but the conversation changed direction and we moved on. A few minutes later I was explaining to him how I'd overreacted to someone calling me Stephen, convinced they knew my name was Steve. That's when he really got my goat.

"So is your name actually Steve then, not Stephen?! He asked.

I shifted uncomfortably in my chair and leant forward. "Are you taking the piss?" I said.

"What do you mean?" Ralph replied.

I genuinely wondered if he thought he was being funny. I repeated my question "Are you taking the piss?" I said firmly. I was fidgeting now; my leg was bouncing, and my face was twitching subconsciously.

"Well normally people called Stephen shorten it to Steve."

I was so wound up! "Seriously, I sit here spilling my guts out to you, telling you things I've never told anyone, and not only do you not know my diagnosis, but you don't even know my fucking name!" I said. There was silence as I waited for him to respond, but he didn't, and we just sat there looking at each other for what seemed a long time before I spoke again.

"What is happening right now?" I demanded, staring intensely into his eyes.

"What do you mean, what's happening?" He responded.

To me it was obvious, but as my therapist I was surprised by his attitude. "You're trying to outstare me, acting the tough guy!" I said.

"No Steve, I'm not trying to outstare you." He replied.

"You're the fucking therapist, you know exactly what's going on here. You're the one trained to read body language, not me. I'm not trained, but even I can see what's happening. I don't know if you think you're handy, and I don't care, but you are giving me the evils and you're pissing me off now!"

Ralph did a good job reassuring me that I'd misread the situation and we finished the session without incident. Turned out he wasn't trying to wind me up after all.

LEVELS OF LUNACY

As a teenager, being called a lunatic was a kind of compliment. "He's a lunatic!" told you that someone was dangerous, mad, or crazy and the only people who fight with lunatics are other lunatics. I had a few friends who were in that category and some might have said I was in there too. At fourteen or fifteen years old, without my mums knowledge I bought myself an air rifle and a tin of pellets. My interests were the military, weight training, weapons, and martial arts. My bedroom didn't have a bed, to save room I just used a mattress on the floor that I leaned against the wall during the day. I had a punchbag hanging from the rafters, a speedball, a weights bench, squat rack, and weights set. I even had a pulley with a loop that I'd put my foot in and hoist almost to the ceiling to help develop high kicks. One night, after reading through one of my army books about sniping I decided to give it a go. Following the instructions in my book I applied camouflage cream to my face, neck and hands before strapping a large diving knife to my right lower leg and sneaking out of the house with my black Weihrauch .22 air rifle. I climbed over the fence of the house behind mine, crept through the back garden, down the side path and jumped the front wall. The house was right next to a school gate, which I quickly scaled then sprinted across the open ground and into the shadows of the buildings. On the other side of the school was the local park and pavilion, and the car park that catered for them was a popular hangout for a group of older kids and young men. They'd park their cars and spend the night drinking, smoking and generally making a nuisance of themselves. I crawled into the school's boundary hedge and got into a position where I could observe them and select some targets. First of all I chose something nice and big, an easy shot to build up some confidence, and shot at a car door that was parked side-on to my location. The car was a typical boy-racer type affair, with a gutless engine, rear spoiler, go-faster stripes, and alloy wheels. The addition of the alloys, the huge speakers that filled the boot and the three passengers in puffa jackets did little to enhance the aesthetics and even less for the performance of the over-laden vehicle. My shot struck the door with a satisfying "Ding" and I watched for a reaction from the men as I broke the barrel and loaded another pellet into the chamber. Their behaviour was already erratic, so it was hard to tell, but at least one of them appeared to react, turning to look towards the noise. For my second shot I thought it would be a good idea to shoot out a window, so I steadied my aim and fired at the front passenger window, again hitting the target with an audible thud, but to my disappointment not smashing the glass. This shot got the attention of a few of them.

"What the fuck was that?" I heard one shout, as he walked around to the side of the car. "Can you guys hear that? I think someone's shooting at us!"

Three or four of them were now inspecting the car and looking around nervously in all directions. I reloaded once more and had another go at the window, failing to smash it again, but succeeding in giving away my location.

"They're over there!" shouted one of the blokes, pointing in my direction and walking towards me.

Five or six others followed his lead and also headed my way, deducing that I was probably in the hedgerow and cautiously making their way across the open grassed area, squatting, and shielding their eyes from the light pollution of the street lights beyond to locate me. It suddenly dawned on me what a precarious position I was in. If I got caught by them I was going to get hurt, badly, if I got caught by the police I was totally screwed and in no position to deny anything with the camouflage cream, knife, and rifle. Heart racing, I crawled back through the hedge and ran as fast as I could back home, taking a short-cut through an old fence and Hawthorn hedgerow, then squeezing through a small gap between some garages that led to the dark alley at the back of my house. I hid my rifle in the garden shed, then quietly went inside through the back door and into the downstairs bathroom where I tried washing off the cam cream with soap and water. To my horror it wouldn't come off, instead the three colours of light green, dark green and brown just merged into a greasy, brown / green paint. Desperate to get it off I went into the kitchen to see what I could find to help me and returned to the bathroom sink with some scouring pads! As far as I'm aware, I am the only person in the world stupid enough to have ever tried this method, and I scrubbed my face with the green, abrasive pad until it was sore. It didn't work, but eventually I got it off after a lot of soap, water, and elbow grease. Luckily, the police never did come round about that incident and the victims never found out it was me either. During recruit training I learned that there is a much easier way to remove cam cream and it involves baby wipes, or shower gel with warm water and lots of lathering. Scouring pads or Scotch Brite are great for cleaning gas parts on weapons but not recommended for skincare.

As a recruit in the Army, being called a lunatic was an insult. "You fucking lunatic!" was the typical response from an instructor when you said or did something they deemed stupid, dangerous, or idiotic. Not cool. I remember the first time I was called a lunatic by my Platoon Sergeant as I lay on the floor, dazed from the impact of my head bouncing off it. That day, between lessons / beastings we had been told to wait in our rooms for the next order. We were always on tenterhooks, waiting to hear the command "Corridor!" or "Outside!" getting screamed from the staff room. Simply going to the toilet during the day was like a deliberate operation and executed in phases because you might get called upon at any point.

Phases of the Op:

1. Listening halt
2. Enter toilet
3. Listening halt
4. Unbuckle trousers
5. Listening halt
6. Rapidly sit down and forcefully excrete as quickly as possible
7. Listening halt
8. Rapidly wipe ass
9. Listening halt
10. Flush and exit stall
11. Listening halt
12. Rapid hand wash and exit toilet
13. Return to room and ensure you have not missed anything

On hearing the command "Outside" we all made our way into the corridor and towards the stairwell to get outside as quickly as possible, only stopping to lock our lockers and place the keys in the box provided. The panic to get outside was probably comparable to what you would see in an office building that was on fire, and the Corporals would be shouting things like "hurry up you fucking people!" warning us "don't be last!" or counting down out loud "ten,......nine,....... eight,... seven........ It worked though because we'd be outside and lined up in three ranks within seconds. This particular time, still in the first few days of training, I slipped on the highly polished floor as I ran down the corridor, landing on my back right outside the staff office, and right in front of the Platoon Sergeant who was shouting angrily in the doorway. The back of my head hit the hard floor with a thud as it whipped backwards, almost knocking me unconscious and those behind jumped over me or dodged sideways in their haste. For a second my vision was blurred as I looked up at the Sergeant a little stunned. My eyes refocused and I saw him looking at me apathetically. In my naivety, I actually thought for a delirious moment that he might be concerned, and was going to ask if I was okay, he must have heard the whack of my skull bashing the ground. I had a lot to learn. "You fucking mong Brown!" he snapped in his broad Scottish accent. "Who told you to lie down in my corridor? Get away you fucking lunatic!... Hurry up!"

As a soldier approaching the end of my career after almost twenty-two years' service, six operational tours, five hundred parachute jumps, and several life threatening experiences, being called a lunatic was more of a diagnosis. When it was first suggested to me that I could have PTSD I was quite dismissive, there were plenty of people who'd had a much harder life than me both civilians and military. After seeing a nurse, psychologist and psychiatrist who all came to the same conclusion I had to consider they might be right. I thought about all the other times I'd received diagnoses from doctors for other ailments and injuries, without questioning their judgement. As well as the usual aches, sprains, and strains that were common language, I'd gladly received doctor's advice when told I had conditions that I'd never even heard of, such as seborrheic dermatitis and plantar fasciitis. I realised the double standards and selective hearing I was employing and accepted that I had PTSD, and the best thing about that was that I could focus on the treatment and embark on my journey towards wellness.

THE DOCTOR DOESN'T ALWAYS KNOW BEST

When I was the Sergeant Major at Pathfinders from 2012-2014, I kept my ear to the ground as best I could to monitor morale amongst the blokes and keep tabs on any personality clashes or rivalries. As you go through the ranks in the army your circle of friends gets smaller and smaller as you must start enforcing the rules and disciplining people, but I always tried to remain approachable to everyone. One day, one of the blokes, a senior Corporal that I'd known for a long time confided in me regarding another soldier. Struggling with his mental health, this bloke had a lot going on. A hard tour of Afghanistan, a life changing physical injury, and the fact he was soon leaving the army were no doubt key factors which affected his psychological state. My mate told me that this soldier, Billy, had told people he was going to kill himself. Without wasting time, I found Billy and asked him to come to my office for a chat and we both sat down to talk. I've never had any training in managing mental health, but I've always been able to talk to people, and have always had a strong paternal instinct for my blokes, so I got to it. "Nobody has told me directly." I lied, not wanting to cause any friction between the blokes. "But I overheard some of the blokes talking, and they were saying that you'd mentioned having suicidal thoughts."

"Yep, that's right." Billy answered directly.

I was surprised by his honesty; I'd anticipated it being much more awkward, but I didn't react that way. "Okay mate, so is that something that has passed or is it something you are still considering as an option?" I asked.

His response seemed honest and genuine and was spoken without emotion. "I'm going to kill the pricks that have fucked me over, and then I'm going to kill myself."

Billy was in my office for an hour and a half, openly explaining how he'd been let down by several people in the MoD and in his personal life and wanted them dead. He was considering a shooting spree followed by suicide and although I didn't know him very well personally, it was obvious to me there was a lot of anger and a lot of sadness in him. I had no reason to doubt his intentions were sincere. Billy loved being in the Pathfinders and his airborne brothers were the only people he trusted. Medically downgraded because of his injuries the prospect of him deploying on operations ever again was bleak so he was leaving. I tried to assure him that I was there for him and so was the Regiment and the Pathfinders. I also spoke to him about seeking help through the Department of Clinical Mental Health (DCMH) who had a permanent facility on our camp. He was adamant that he wanted nothing to do with the medical system that he believed had failed him already and the only support he needed was to see his time out with his mates at Pathfinders.

After our long chat we shook hands and Billy left. I walked straight into the boss's office next door where the Officer Commanding Pathfinders sat at his desk. I shut the door and briefed him on what Billy had told me and my concerns for his wellbeing. We both agreed this needed to be handled carefully and that we should seek guidance from a higher authority. I knew of someone in Brigade Headquarters who was responsible for the welfare of injured personnel and suggested calling her. The boss agreed and encouraged me to back up the call with an email. I emailed first then phoned the appointed person. They answered and the call began like this.

"Hello, my name is Sergeant Major Steve Brown from the Pathfinders. I'd like to get some advice on how to deal with a situation regarding one of my soldiers who has just confessed to me that he wants to commit suicide."

"Is it Billy?" they asked.

"Erm, yes, it is actually." I replied, rather surprised by the quick assumption.

"He's been saying that for ages!" they said nonchalantly. "He won't do it! He's just really angry, he won't kill himself."

I went on to explain that I wasn't convinced and thought he needed help, but they weren't interested. I got nowhere. They offered nothing.

The next place I tried was the DCMH which was a short bike ride away. I walked into the building and spoke to the receptionist, who, despite me not having an appointment, arranged for me to speak to one of the staff. After briefing that lady on my dilemma, she explained that they could not take "walk-in" patients and Billy would have to be referred to them by a doctor from the Medical Centre. She was as helpful as she could be, but unfortunately there were procedures that had to be followed.

After booking an appointment at the Medical Centre I got to see a doctor who I also briefed about Billy and my failed efforts with the other establishments. He listened intently then gave me his advice.

"Tell him to come to Sick Parade tomorrow morning and I will have a chat with him." He offered.

"He won't go sick Sir." I replied. He won't come to the Med Centre, he hates doctors!"

"Then why don't *you* book him an appointment and order him to come here?" he proposed. "Not coming would be missing a parade and that would get him in trouble." He explained, knowing that a soldier could get charged for missing a parade, so that threat might force him to attend.

"I can't do that! I'm one of the few people he trusts!" I said. "He won't come and I'm certainly not going to charge him!"

I think the doc was trying to help, but didn't grasp the contempt Billy held them in. For all I know he was on his hit list.

"There's only one other option." He said. "Section him!"

"Section him! Jesus Christ, really?" I replied. "Who would that be done by?"

"You! You'd have to do it!" the doc answered, pointing at me.

I couldn't think of anything worse. After the conversation I'd had with Billy, where he'd spilled his guts out to me, telling me he believed I had his back, that the Pathfinders were the only people he trusted, the only place he felt safe. That scenario could never happen, it would be the ultimate betrayal, it would destroy him. I left that appointment without resolution too. The boss and I kept trying to find help for Billy and I was posted out of the Pathfinders before he left, but as far as I know he is now a civilian and as yet, has not gone on a shooting spree.

-PSYCHOTHERAPY-

MY DOG GOT MURDERED

My first family pet, that was part of my life from infancy was a beautiful little Sheltie dog called Lassie. She stayed with us after my dad left when I was about 6 months old, and we all loved her to bits. I remember how she would stop me running around the house by biting onto the back of my clothes and pulling me backwards. At some point my mum got involved with a bloke called Terry and at some point, he became a complete nut case that terrorised us. My mum always said that he was alright until he started taking drugs, but then he went crazy. One day he took Lass out for a walk and returned without her. He said she'd died while they were walking, and he'd dug a grave and buried her in a field. We never saw her again, dead, or alive. That sick bastard killed my dog. We all knew it, and I remember crying my eyes out, I must have been five or six years old. During one of my EMDR sessions, that event came up in another vision where the lines between what happened and what I imagined are blurred, and although I can't remember how the session began or ended, I do remember a significant part.

Sat in the back of a car my brother and I were scared. I was on the left, leaning over to my right, to see through the gap between the front seats. My brother was on the right side, leant forward, holding on to the sides of the driver's seat in front of him. We were both looking through the front windscreen nervously, as if expecting to see something bad. My mum was in the driver's seat doing the same, leaning forwards with her hands on the top of the steering wheel, her fingers fidgetily squeezing the black plastic trim. The fear in the atmosphere was oppressive as sporadic sobs and sharp inward breaths added to the tension. Then a man appeared ahead, slowly walking towards us, just out of focus.

"Do you get a sense of who it is walking towards you in that car?" Dr Jackson asked.

My heart was pounding as I was immersed in the image, feeling the anxiety and fear of that young boy. I concentrated on the image, not knowing who it represented until he looked up and I saw his face. "It's my mums' ex-boyfriend Terry." I said with a mixture of sadness and anger. Now I knew what all the worry was about. The anxiety grew as we kept watching, then my brother shouted out. "Where's Lass? Where is she?"

We were all crying now as Terry continued to walk towards us nonchalantly. Lass was gone, and he was so brazen, he hadn't even kept her lead to pretend he'd accidentally lost her. We were trapped in a car and he was coming for us next. Dr Jackson listened as I described the scene in detail and asked me if there was maybe someone who might come to our rescue. It could be anyone, a family member, a friend, even a fictional superhero but as much as I wanted someone to spring to mind nobody did, and we continued. A figure approached the car on the passenger side, but I couldn't see their face because the car roof blocked it, all I could see was the middle part of their body. It was obviously a man, and they wore a cream white shirt with the sleeves rolled down ¾ of the way and matching trousers. The fear subsided but the sadness remained as the man pulled the door open and leant down in the car doorway. We were rescued, a man had come to save us, but it wasn't Superman, or even my dad, it was an adult version of me. I still find it really sad recounting these sessions, because it makes me realise how helpless I must have felt back then, I think I just wanted to be bigger and stronger so I could protect us, because nobody else was going to do it.

-CHAPTER THIRTEEN-

NEVER FORGOTTEN

CORPORAL BRYAN BUDD V.C

An event that I think disproportionately affected me psychologically is the death of my good friend Bryan Budd V.C, who was tragically killed in Helmand Province, Afghanistan in August 2006. Even though I wasn't involved in the mission where he was killed nor the follow up mission that discovered and retrieved his body, I feel immense sadness when I think about him and the circumstances in which he died, which is often. In the days after his death, I spoke to some friends who had been involved in those missions, one of which I knew very well as I had joined the army and gone through recruit training with him. Like all soldiers who worked with Bryan they were full of praise for his leadership and soldiering skills but kept their emotions to themselves as they talked about the scene where he was found. I wonder how they really felt at that time and how they have coped with it since. In my dining room, there is a framed picture of Bry which hangs proudly on the wall. It is a limited-edition print, from a painting by the artist Stuart Brown, and it depicts him firing his weapon while charging towards the Taliban fighters who killed him. I look at that picture every day and feel a mixture of pride and sadness. Proud to have known and served with him, that he cemented himself in Parachute Regiment history, that he earned the highest award for valour possible in the British Army. At the same time, I feel sad that his wife Lorena lost such an amazing bloke, that his children Isobel and Imogen have had to grow up without their dad, that he died alone in that horrible place, and selfishly, that I will never see him again. While writing about Bry, I have had to take several breaks because whenever I think about him, or look at his picture for a long time, I get extremely sad and have to distract myself before I start crying. I cannot imagine how awful it must be for his family, it must be absolutely horrendous for them. My picture of Bry was presented to me as a leaving gift from a place I worked from 2007-2011 and was a complete surprise. I'd already been presented with the standard gift of a large survival knife, chromed, and mounted on wood so I wasn't expecting it at all. I kept my thankyou speech short because I was welling up. I don't mind admitting stuff like that because I am well over the bravado and macho bullshit that some thrive on, and some expect from soldiers. There's definitely a time and place for stoicism and the old "stiff upper lip," especially in the armed forces, but I've come to realise that there's also a time for reflection and grieving.

Bry was a great bloke. We knew each other from 3 Para and had a fantastic relationship. We served in the Pathfinders together for several years and deployed on tours together. Bry was my Patrol Medic in Iraq when I was a Patrol Commander and I took a lot of confidence from him being there, because he ran our medical training, and I knew he would be mega if we took any casualties. He was always mucking about, never taking things too seriously and would always greet me in a strong German accent with the phrase "Brown hates all officers!" when we hadn't seen each other for a while. That was his impression from a 1970's World War Two movie called Cross of Iron, where the main character is a German Army Corporal called "Steiner." As a young soldier I had a strong dislike of officers and in the movie, there's a scene where two officers are talking about Steiner's attitude, when one says, "Steiner hates all officers!" That tickled Bry, and despite the fact he was comparing me to a Nazi soldier I liked our private joke too. One time when we deployed on tour at short notice Bry was on holiday abroad. He'd gone to South America to explore and to see Macchu Pichu in Peru, so our headquarters did their best to get a message to him and we prepared our equipment and left camp. In his absence, one of the other blokes went into Bry's room and packed his kit for him. In Pathfinders our kit was always packed and ready to go because we were permanently on high readiness, so it was just a quick check to ensure the essentials were there and his kit was loaded up with everyone else's. Luckily for him the blokes in the Pathfinders were relatively mature and didn't stitch him up by packing his rucksack full of useless items. When I was in 3 Para, peoples kit would regularly get sabotaged. One of my mates once had his sleeping bag exchanged for a crusty old blanket when we were in Norway, on the same night we were building and sleeping in snow-hole survival shelters. He had a rough night! We also had a heavy old iron in one of my platoons that we used to hide in each other's bergans. Everyone would know who had it, and if you deployed with it, you'd have to bring it back. If you didn't everyone would know you'd ditched a bit of kit and jeopardised the security of your team by leaving evidence behind.

Soldiers deploying on operations were always processed through the Air Mounting Centre (AMC) at South Cerney in Gloucestershire, a laborious procedure that I never understood. We would go there prior to going to RAF Brize Norton and spend hours sitting around until it was our turn to show our passports to some army Corporal in a high-vis jacket and get our kit weighed. The kit would then get put back on the truck it had come off and we'd sit around again until it was time to go get on a plane. When we arrived at Brize Norton, we'd do exactly the same thing again, this time to RAF people in high-vis. I still don't understand why we had to do it twice.

The next time I saw Bry was while we were waiting in the AMC. Writing it down, makes me question how accurate this memory is because it sounds unlikely and it was a long time ago, but this is how I remember it. He turned up with a beard, wearing long shorts, a short-sleeved safari shirt and sandals, and I remember him standing in a doorway as we all looked up to see him stood there smiling broadly. He looked like a poorly disguised CIA agent from Columbia. Everyone else was dressed in camouflage with polished boots and clean-shaven faces. One of the other blokes gave Bry his kit and he quickly got washed and changed after exchanging greetings with his mates. Later that day Bry told me he'd been given the message to call our Sergeant Major by the hotel reception staff at his hotel in the middle of nowhere after returning from an excursion. After learning about our impending deployment, he'd sought transport to the nearest airfield to catch a flight to an international airport. Because he was in a remote area, part of his journey was on the back of a donkey and he told me how he'd been riding through tracks and trails sat on top of it shouting "Yah, yah!" like a cowboy, trying to make it run faster. He made it on time so it must have worked.

Bry was a good-looking bloke and a lot of people used to say he looked like Joey from the T.V show "Friends" He'd even play along by using Joey's catchphrase "How you doin?" One night we were in a pub in Ipswich together when we got talking to some girls. Even though paratroopers get extremely angered by people who pretend to be from our Regiment, we are pretty good at pretending ourselves, and that is because we know a lot of women have a negative perception about us. So, Bry told the one he was with that he was a nurse, and I said I was a fireman. They were suspicious and questioned us. Bry pulled it off because he knew loads about medicine and medical procedures from his work in Pathfinders, running the Medical cell, and I pulled it off because I'm really good at talking shit.

SERGEANT JON HOLLOINGSWORTH CGC, QGM

In November 2006 I was a rear passenger in a car driving back to the parachute centre in El Centro, California, USA when I checked my phone for any messages. I never used my mobile for calls when I was abroad back then because it was so expensive, but I did do one or two texts a day. I turned it on and put it down on the seat between my legs so it could boot-up and search for a signal and after a couple of minutes it sprung to life, vibrating and beeping. I had a few missed calls and a text. The text was from an old 3 Para mate called Stu, who'd recently had a leg blown off in Afghanistan, and it read:

"Have you seen the news about the British soldier in Iraq? I think the bloke they're talking about is Jon H."

I hadn't read a newspaper or seen any UK news for over a week, just CNN and Fox News channels. I also had a missed call from a different friend called Lennie, who worked in the SF with Jon. I tried to suppress my immediate negative thoughts, but it was unusual to hear from either of these blokes, let alone both of them in the same day. I asked the others in the car if they had heard anything in the news about British soldiers and they hadn't. I called Lennie to see what was going on and he answered promptly.

"Hello mate, have you heard what has happened?" he said solemnly.

It was obviously bad, but I hoped it wasn't the worst. "No mate, I'm in El Centro, I haven't heard anything, please don't tell me he's dead." I said hopefully.

"Sorry mate, but yes he's been killed on ops. I wanted to let you know because I know you are good friends." Lennie told me. That must have been as horrible for him to say as it was for me to hear.

"Fucks sake." I sighed. I didn't ask for details, things like that can't be discussed over the phone. "Thanks for telling me mate. I appreciate that. I hope you're alright."

Our chat was brief and shortly afterwards I was throwing myself out of an airplane for the second time that day. The last time I spoke to Jon was when he was back in the UK recovering from getting shot in the back of the neck on another mission in Iraq. The bullet missed his carotid artery by millimetres and left a hole in his helmet and he was sent home to recover. Even though he was given the option to stay in the UK, he was keen to get back out with his team, and selflessly went back out to finish the tour with his Squadron. That decision proved fatal when he was shot again during another raid and died shortly afterwards. Jon had already been awarded the Queens Gallantry Medal (QGM) for work in Northern Ireland and he was posthumously awarded the Conspicuous Gallantry Cross (CGC) for his outstanding bravery in Iraq. Awesome soldier.

John and I knew each other for years but became good friends when we were both in Wales training for SAS selection. There were about ten blokes preparing for the course but after a couple of days, we realised that we both wanted to do the same kind of training and partnered up, sharing our knowledge of the hills and potential routes that might be used on the course. We spent about eight hours a day walking up and down those hills, through boggy marshes, and searching for goat tracks across the Brecon Beacons and Elan Valley, and had a good laugh all the way round every route. Jon was from Patrols Platoon and very fit and knowledgeable about everything to do with soldiering, but he was also very humble. To be fair, I learned a whole lot more from him than he got from me, but we enjoyed each other's company and covered a vast area.

I remember Jon telling me during one of our marches about how he'd previously attended the Pathfinder Selection Cadre and been unimpressed by some of the instructors. He'd actually withdrawn himself from the course voluntarily after one of the test marches, because of the way he'd been treated, along with another soldier from 3 Para Patrols Platoon who also ended up in the SAS. They'd both arrived at a checkpoint together, and the instructor had talked to them with utter contempt as he gave them their next set of coordinates. Jon and Matt had both confirmed the location on their maps when the instructor asked arrogantly. "Hollingsworth, what's the motto of the Pathfinder Platoon?" Jon told me that he looked across the small tent towards Matt, and they both shook their heads despondently.

"First in." he answered, disinterestedly.

"That's right. Now fuck off!" the instructor replied, quickly pulling the zip of his tent closed. Jon and Matt finished the test, then withdrew themselves from the course.

That story stuck with me, and a couple of years later while I was on Pathfinder selection, I had a similar experience with a jumped-up instructor but got talked out of withdrawing by a friend called Gareth, who was an officer also attending the course. We both agreed that if we passed, we would never treat future applicants like we'd been treated by a minority of the instructors and a few years after that, I was running the course and he was in Special Forces. I was firm but fair as an instructor and never spoke to anyone the way Jon and I had been spoken to. When I was the Pathfinder Platoon Sergeant, I used Jon's example to demonstrate how we could spoil opportunities to recruit awesome soldiers if we acted disrespectfully.

On the last day of our training in Wales, Jon and I were navigating the final leg of our route on a mountain called Fan Fawr, when I ran down a small mound and fell over. The white minibus we'd parked in a layby earlier that morning was clearly visible, as we covered the last couple of kilometres of the relatively short, twenty-one-kilometre route. Jon laughed as I fell on my arse, but quickly stopped and came to my aid when he realised I was injured. I knew it was bad because I'd had several ankle injuries before. It was about two weeks until Selection started, and it really hurt. "I'm fucked mate!" I said to Jon.

"Fuck off mate, you'll be alright!" He assured me.

I knew it was a bad one, I'd heard it pop and it was extremely painful. I was devastated. "I've really fucked it mate!" I told him. Jon was mega and helped me back to the minibus, but it I'd torn the ligament in my ankle and had to rest it for several weeks.

Jon attended the course as planned, but he broke his ankle jumping off the vehicle after one of the first test marches and got withdrawn. As soon as it healed he went back on the course and passed with flying colours.

SERGEANT NICK BROWN

Parachute Regiment battalions are blessed with hundreds of excellent soldiers, but there are some that are acknowledged as the best of the best. I call them the "Super soldiers" because they are known and respected by the soldiers and officers alike for their awesome skills. Everyone wants them in their section, platoon, company or battalion and they always perform well on every course or deployment. One such soldier was Nick Brown, and I first heard about him from a couple of friends in Pathfinders who had served with him in battalion. He was a senior Corporal in 2 Para, who had influenced them during their time there, and now he was attending our course to become a Pathfinder. They were both one hundred percent confident that he would pass and looked forward to the capabilities he would bring to enhance our unit. Based on what they'd said, I was excited to meet him, and hoped he would get through the course without injury, which seemed the only thing that would stop him. He smashed the course, passed as "Top Student," and became a hugely popular member of the Pathfinders. I worked with Nick on tour in Iraq, and he was every bit as good as I thought he'd be, cool, calm under pressure and full of great ideas that he could draw from his experience.

When in camp, at dinner time all the living-in soldiers would sit together at a big table and spin stories until everyone else had left and we were eventually asked to leave by the cleaning staff. The most prolific storyteller by a mile, was Nick, and he'd have us all laughing out loud most evenings as he recounted hilarious tales from his past with great enthusiasm and animation. I remember one day he was explaining how he'd been taught how to teach, by using as many of the senses as possible. His story was about a memory game he'd done on a course called a Kims game. The instructor placed ten items on the floor under a blanket, then revealed them for sixty seconds while the students tried to memorise them before recovering them. Nick and the others then had a further minute to write down everything they had seen. This game is commonly used in the Army as a concurrent activity to keep soldiers entertained during periods of inactivity and is a lot more difficult than it sounds. Nick described how the results ranged with some scoring better than others like normal and then explained how the instructor made his point on using the senses. One of the items was a spoon.

"What's this?" the instructor asked the course.

"A spoon." One of them answered.

"Yes, it's a spoon. But what's special about this spoon? Why is this spoon so memorable?"

Nick described how there was silence as the students tried to see something notable, but there was nothing unique about the piece of cutlery, it was just a standard spoon. Nick became more and more animated, and a wry smile appeared on his face as he told how the instructor continued.

"If you want to remember it, you need to do more than just see it! You have to smell it, to hear it as it.." Nick stood up at this point and got really loud as he acted out what the instructor had done..... "As it stabs you in the eye! Oouucchh! It hurts so bad! I can feel the cold steel stabbing into my eyeball, and the warm salty blood running down my cheek and into my mouth, and as I pull it out I hear it go pop, as my eye is torn from its socket! Aahhh, it's so painful!"

After that the instructor did the game again with ten new items and according to Nick, the results were much better when using his imaginative technique.

In the days before "Spoiler alert!" was a thing, I needed to be given one prior to another story. Nick spent two years as an instructor at Depot Para, turning clueless civilians into paratroopers over six months of the most arduous training in the British Army. Reminiscing about a lesson he'd given to the recruits, Nick was talking about the "Noise and light demo" which is delivered during the first field exercise that recruits conduct. I remember receiving that lesson to this day, because I was so impressed by the skills of my Depot instructors.

That day in June 1993, I was sat with the rest of my recruit platoon amongst the grass and ferns at the top of a hill, on the Army training area. One of the Corporals was about to teach us the importance of noise and light discipline, and why using hand signals, dressing correctly, and minimising the use of torchlight was vitally important to the operational effectiveness of an infantry unit. Before the demo began the Corporal explained to us that one of the other instructors was going to try and sneak up on us during the class.

"Using the camouflage and concealment techniques that we taught you earlier, Cpl Jones will start from the bottom of the hill and see how close he can get to this location without being seen or heard." he said. "If at any time any of you think you have seen him, or hear him, raise your hand and point to where he is." He called out to the instructor below, "Cpl Jones, are you ready?"

"Ready!" came the distant reply.

"Exercise begin!" our instructor shouted.

For the next twenty minutes we learned how sounds like the rustling of waterproof clothing, whispering voices, and weapons being cocked carried through the forest and open spaces. Coffee was boiled upwind, and a cloth doused in cheap aftershave was laid out to demonstrate how scents travelled, and we saw how different textures and equipment reflected natural or manmade light. At the end of the demo the instructor asked if anyone had seen or heard Cpl Jones approaching, and nobody had.

Shouting into the open ground beyond us he said, "Corporal Jones, wherever you are, can you stand up please?"

Silently, Corporal Jones rose up from the ground about ten feet away from us like some kind of Ninja, and we all stared at him in awe. I was well impressed, but not surprised, the Corporals were like superheroes to me.

Ten years had passed since then when Nick recounted the time he'd taught the same lesson to his recruits. I was devasted when he explained how they'd place a well camouflaged instructor amongst the ferns prior to the recruits arriving and get another Corporal to shout "Ready" from the bottom.
"No way! Is that really what happens?" I asked him.
"Yes of course it is mate, didn't you know that? That's an old classic that is." He told me.
"For fucks sake, I really thought they'd done it. I can't believe you've told me that, I'm gutted now!" I admitted. I felt cheated, and gullible.
We both laughed at my naivety. My instructors were still Ninjas though.
Nick passed SAS Selection after being promoting to Sergeant in the Pathfinders and was sadly killed on Special Forces operations in Baghdad in March 2008.

Printed in Great Britain
by Amazon

85316152R00142